THE
RED BADGE
OF COURAGE
REDEFINING THE HERO

TWAYNE'S MASTERWORK STUDIES
Robert Lecker, General Editor

THE
RED BADGE
OF COURAGE
REDEFINING THE HERO

Donald B. Gibson

TWAYNE PUBLISHERS • BOSTON
A Division of G.K. Hall & Co.

The Red Badge of Courage: Redefining the Hero

Donald B. Gibson

Twayne's Masterwork Studies No. 15

Copyright 1988 by G.K. Hall & Co.
All rights reserved.
Published by Twayne Publishers
A division of G.K. Hall & Co.
70 Lincoln Street, Boston, Massachusetts 02111

Typeset in 11/14 Sabon by
Compset, Inc., of Beverly, Massachusetts

Printed on permanent/durable acid-free paper
and bound in the United States of America

First Printing

Library of Congress Cataloging-in-Publication Data

Gibson, Donald B.
The Red badge of courage : redefining the hero / Donald B. Gibson.
p.   cm. — (Twayne's masterwork studies ; no. 15)
Bibliography: p.
Includes index.
ISBN 0-8057-7961-2 (alk. paper) ISBN 0-8057-8014-9 (pbk. : alk. paper)
1. Crane, Stephen, 1871–1900. Red badge of courage. 2. United States—History—Civil War, 1861–1865—Literature and the war.
3. Heroes in literature. 4. Courage in literature. I. Title.
II. Series.
PS1449.C85R3945   1988
813'.4—dc 19

87-27967
CIP

To Hyatt Waggoner and R. W. Stallman,
two master critics

Contents

Note on References and Acknowledgments

The text I have used is the most complete and reliable text of *The Red Badge of Courage* suitable for classroom use: the Signet Classic edition (New American Library, 1960). There are other good texts, but none is more thorough and detailed in its editing than that of the late R. W. Stallman, the dean of Crane critics and scholars, and the man who has done more to create and sustain the modern critical revival of interest in the life and works of Stephen Crane than anyone else. Page references to that text are noted parenthetically in the pages following.

Grateful acknowledgment is made to the libraries and librarians of Rutgers, Princeton, and Columbia universities and to the curators of the Crane collection of the Newark Public Library, especially for their supplying the photograph of the bust of Stephen Crane for the frontispiece of this volume.

Stephen Crane (1871–1900)
Bust by Stephen McNeely.
Photo from Newark Public Library, Newark, N.J.

Chronology:
Stephen Crane's Life and Works

1871	Born 1 November, Newark, New Jersey. Parents: the Reverend Jonathan Townley Crane, a Methodist minister, and Mary Helen Peck Crane. The Reverend Crane is presiding elder for the Newark district of the Methodist Church.
1878	Moves to Port Jervis, New York, from Paterson, New Jersey (1876), scene of Whilomville tales. Begins school.
1880	Father, Jonathan Townley Crane, dies.
1883	After several moves and brief sojourns in and around Port Jervis, Mrs. Crane moves with him to Asbury Park, New Jersey.
1888	Enrolls in Hudson River Institute (formerly Claverack College) in New York.
1890	Enters Lafayette College, Easton, Pennsylvania. Joins Delta Upsilon fraternity. Leaves after one term.
1891	Enters Syracuse University. Works as city correspondent for *New York Tribune*. Devotes himself to athletics, primarily baseball. Publishes first story, "The King's Favor," in the *University Herald*. Writes first draft of *Maggie*. Decides to become a writer. Does not return to college in the fall and works for brother Townley at Asbury Park as reporter. Mother dies in December.
1892	Final revision of *Maggie* in fall. Settles (see below) in New York, writing and sleeping where he can after having commuted there often from Asbury Park and from his brother Edmund's house in Lakeview, New Jersey. During this time he frequents and begins to know the Bowery and some of its residents. He lives for a while at the Pendennis Club, a "pad" for Bohemian students. Works briefly for *New York Tribune* and *Herald*. Five "Sullivan County Sketches" published in *Tribune*.

1893   Publishes *Maggie: A Girl of the Streets* under the pseudonym, Johnston Smith. *The Red Badge of Courage* begun. Questions Civil War veterans in Virginia about the war.

1894   *The Red Badge* published in installments in abridged form in newspaper, the *Philadelphia Press*. First poetry written. *George's Mother* begun. Several tales and sketches published.

1895   Irving Bacheller, head of syndicate that serialized *The Red Badge*, is so impressed with novel that he sends Crane west and to Mexico to write anything Crane wishes for the Bacheller news syndicate. First volume of poetry *The Black Riders* published. *The Red Badge* published in its entirety. *The Third Violet* written. *Maggie* reissued under Crane's own name. Goes to Florida to report on filibustering expeditions to Cuba for Bacheller syndicate. Meets Cora Howarth Taylor, with whom he later lives as though married.

1897   Shipwrecked off Florida coast as he attempts to get to Cuba. The experience forms basis for "The Open Boat" published in June. Sails to Europe to cover Greco-Turkish War via London and Paris with Cora. Returns in June to London. The experience results in a novel, *Active Service*. Writes "The Monster," "The Bride Comes to Yellow Sky," "Death and the Child," *The Third Violet*. Moves with Cora to Oxted, Surrey. Meets Joseph Conrad.

1898   Attempts to volunteer for service during Spanish-American War. Rejected. Hired by Pulitzer as war correspondent in Cuba and Puerto Rico. Delivers excellent dispatches. *The Open Boat and Other Tales of Adventure* published in April. Several major short stories written the year before are published this year. Returns finally to New York in November.

1899   Returns to England where Cora has prepared a residence at Brede Place, Sussex. Begins writing desperately to pay off debts. *War Is Kind*, his second volume of verse. Also *Active Service* and *The Monster and Other Stories*. Stricken by massive tubercular hemorrhage at Christmastime.

1900   *Whilomville Stories, Wounds in the Rain.* Last novel *The O'Ruddy* begun. *Great Battles of the World* written and published the following year. *The O'Ruddy*, his last novel, finished posthumously by Robert Barr and published in 1903. Dies of tuberculosis at the age of twenty-eight in a sanitorium in Badenweiler, Germany, on 5 June. Buried in Hillside, New Jersey.

1

Historical Context

The difference between *The Red Badge of Courage* and any American novel written before it is a measure of its author's extraordinary imaginative capacities, of the uniqueness of his vision, of his daring to pursue paths untried by others. Yet, despite its contrast to the work of American authors preceding him and its difference from the work of his contemporaries, the novel is nonetheless a product of its times and ahead of its time. It is at one with its time because Crane responded to his era in ways that anticipated twentieth-century thought. It is ahead of its time in the sense that it does not conform to very many contemporary notions about what literature should be and do.

Crane is a harbinger, one of those few nineteenth-century writers (joining the company of Emily Dickinson and Walt Whitman) whose work seems responsible for making twe···ieth-century American literature what it turned out to be. He seems to have seen to the core of his time, to have sensed the very essence of his century that would carry on into the next. He was truly a genius (even though he was not able to finish college). He was a genius in his choice of subjects; in his use of language—unique, unusually creative, and new; in his understanding and interpretation of his culture during his time, including an intuitive grasp of the prevailing philosophical currents of his age.

He was one of very few writers who felt that people and concerns other than those of the very rich or the middle class were appropriate subjects of literature. The genteel character of nineteenth-century literature was responsible for dictating that only certain subjects and hence only certain characters could legitimately belong to literary expression. Hence Crane's first novel, *Maggie: A Girl of the Streets,* was shocking to many because its characters are lower-class denizens of New York's Bowery and the chief character, Maggie, descends into prostitution. Several of his earlier stories, such as "The Man in the Storm" and "An Experiment in Misery," concern characters who are street people, homeless, without jobs or significant social station. When he wrote about seemingly traditional subjects, they were, as he perceived them, likely to be not very traditional at all or at least questionably so.

Crane's language moves toward the language of twentieth-century literature more than any other nineteenth-century author's. It is not that his language directly influenced other writers (though it probably did more in poetry than in prose) so much as that his unusual usage freed the language of literature from the bonds of what had hardened through the nineteenth century into a "literary language" that was highly restrictive. Crane's characters speak a language appropriate to their socioeconomic class and the particular circumstances in which they find themselves. His narrators speak colorfully and in unusually creative ways. The unique and odd character of his language caused him to be parodied frequently.

When *The Red Badge of Courage* was being written, the latter part of the nineteenth century, the nation was undergoing the greatest growth and expansion since its inception. It was the time when the great American fortunes either had been made or were being consolidated. Rockefeller, J. P. Morgan, Carnegie, Leland Stanford, and others were self-made men who, through shrewdness, cunning, daring, and skill, made vast fortunes that would have been unimaginable in other times and places. The huge profits accrued by financiers and manufacturers during the Civil War made money readily available for investment in other profit-making ventures. The incredible progress in technology and manufacturing, and the widespread movement of goods and materials, lay at the base of this era known to us as "the Gilded Age," a time of unbridled materialism and lust for profits through the practice of laissez-faire capitalism.

The Red Badge reflects its time in an obverse way. When the American nation at large had its eyes focused on the world and on the profit it might bring, focused on the seemingly endless supply of natural resources and on the technology and manpower (from immigration) to exploit them; when the American nation was beginning to feel like the powerful giant among nations that it would become, Stephen Crane turned his focus inward, away from the world at large and toward the effect of those gigantic and complex forces on the individual person and the human psyche.

We see this phenomenon on two levels: in the style of Crane's writing, and in his subjects and themes. In *The Red Badge* the seeming peculiarity of the style reflects the author's highly subjective and personalized mode of expression, frequently described as "impressionistic." Because the novel focuses on the internal workings of Henry Fleming's psyche, it is not a war novel in any sense; rather, it is a study of its main character's reactions and responses in a wartime situation. The whole of the novel's technical point of view, the third-person limited point of view, reflects the author's focus on the private experience of his main character rather than upon the external world.

Crane, as did nearly all his contemporaries, knew about Charles Darwin and was attuned to many of the implications of Darwinism in connection with the general tenor of the times. He knew, for example, that traditional moral and social values were called into question if the universe were what Darwin's scheme implied it to be in *The Origin of Species,* published in America in 1860. Such an understanding clearly is the source of the themes of most of Crane's poetry in its many reversals of traditional belief and sentiment. Surely the countless comparisons of human characters and actions to those of animals in *The Red Badge* and elsewhere owe their existence to Crane's awareness of the implications of Darwinism. The meaning of the novel itself is inseparable from Crane's interpretation of the meaning of Darwinism insofar as it bears upon human values.

Crane's willingness to experiment with language and form reflects his awareness that his times called for new modes of perception and expression. In his literature and in his life Crane was anything but a conformist. While other writers of his time—Longfellow, Lowell, Whittier—were writing in conventional ways about conventional subjects, Crane was questioning tradition in literature, in social rule and regulation, in morals, in philosophy. His unwillingness to follow the rules of convention was responsible for his unsavory reputation as a drug addict, an alcoholic, and consort of prostitutes. At the same time, his unwillingness to conform to conventional dictates made it possible for him to write in new and exciting ways, unconstrained by literary convention, unfettered by the past.

2

The Importance of the Work

The Red Badge of Courage is the pivotal American work standing between the nineteenth and twentieth centuries; it divides the two eras. In his review of the novel (*New York Times*, 26 January 1896) the novelist Harold Frederick says of Crane's work: "If there were in existence any books of a similar character, one could start confidently by saying that it is the best of its kind. But it has no fellows. It is a book outside of all classification." And so it is—or so it was. We are by now used to all manner of literary experiment, and the book therefore cannot begin to seem as new to us as it appeared to its first readers.

The Red Badge demonstrated what a twentieth-century consciousness "feels" like in its depiction of two minds, two consciousnesses focused upon experience—the one Henry Fleming's, the other the narrator's, both struggling to make some sense out of things. Henry's is the less comprehensive consciousness since he has no access to the narrator's though the narrator has ready access to his. Both consciousnesses are limited, Henry's by the restrictions placed upon him by circumstance (we can only, as Henry, see what we can see); the narrator's by choosing to restrict his view to Henry and what Henry sees. The point of the restrictions of perspective is to be true to life experience. If our knowledge is limited both by the physical limitations of our vision, our inability to know with certainty anything beyond that which we experience, and if our understanding of our experience is shaped and colored by our psyches, then *how* can we truly know and *what* can we truly know? This is the dilemma faced by people in the twentieth century, a dilemma that arose out of growing lack of certainty, as the nineteenth century came to a close, about the status of institutional authority. And this is the dilemma described to us in fictional terms by Crane's text. In seeing it dramatized we are in a better position to understand the problems posed by the subjectivity of human experience. It is remarkable that Crane was able even to *grasp* the problem, much less to articulate it.

On a less complex level the novel deals with the perennial problem of maturation and the individual's relation to authority. This is obviously a universal problem, but it has its particular American applications. Insofar as the principles of freedom and independence have any real relation to American character, those principles mean the right of the individual not to be imposed upon by authority. Certainly the question of authority is dealt with directly by all of our major nineteenth-century writers, and this preoccupation has specifically to do with our history, our connection initially with England as a parent figure and our subsequent rebellion and attempt to establish ourselves as parent. Thus we may trace this theme of *The Red Badge of Courage* at least as far back as Hawthorne, Melville, Emerson, Thoreau, and Whitman, and even further.

Probably the chief reason that we continue to read and study *The Red Badge* is that it is an inexhaustible source of literary sustenance. We can never devour it, we can never finish it because it will not digest. The novel undercuts itself. It says there is no answer to the questions it raises; yet it says the opposite. It says there is an answer to the questions it raises; yet it says the opposite. It says that Henry Fleming finally sees things as they are; it says he is a deluded fool. It says that Henry does not see things as they are; but no one else does either.

Henry begins the novel by understanding his situation in fictional terms, in terms of myth and fairytale. By the end of the novel Henry sees things differently, but simply in terms of another myth—a more modern one of the meaning of heroism. In one way this is good. In another it is simply another delusion. In one sense, Henry's belief that he has achieved the status of hero is undercut by the view of the narrator that even the concept of heroism in war is a delusion; in another sense, even the narrator's view of Henry is not to be relied upon, for it constitutes its own fiction. The narrator has no more real or solid basis on which to ground his sense of reality than does Henry. None of the possible views of actuality proposed by the novel is finally and unequivocally denied except the view that nature is other than indifferent to the plight and situation of people. This is the kind of thinking that engages the modern mind. The question is not whether Crane is right; but whether he puts forth considerations worth entertaining. Clearly he does.

In interpreting the novel the reader must face a challenge: to make sense of whatever interpretation one chooses without violating the text. We cannot decide that Henry is or is not a hero in the eyes of the author without dealing with the contrary experience. The final question always is, What does the text say? It is always tempting to fall into the cleverest of literary traps: to assume the perspective of the ("perhaps," in this case) duped protagonist. Crane makes it easy to become Henry Fleming if the reader wants to do that. Such complexity and flexibility of mind force similar complex and flexible responses from the attentive and cooperative reader; and such responses keep, and will continue to keep, *The Red Badge of Courage* alive as a major work of American literature.

3

Critical Reception

When *The Red Badge of Courage* burst upon the literary scene in October of 1895, few people knew who Stephen Crane was. Six months later everyone who had the least pretension to knowledge of modern letters not only knew who he was but probably had an opinion of some kind about the man and his work. Few people, either reviewers or readers, sustained a neutral attitude toward Stephen Crane, toward any of his work that was available during the six months preceding and following the initial publication of *The Red Badge of Courage*. *Maggie: A Girl of the Streets* was republished in late May 1896 after having been first privately printed by Crane in 1893; *The Black Riders,* his first collection of poems, was published a few months prior to the war novel on 11 May 1895.

Every one of these volumes provoked controversy because each of them, in some way or another, flew directly in the face of tradition, and it is clear from reading the responses to Crane's work that, to a great degree commentators evaluated it largely in terms of their own sense of the extent to which literature should be governed by tradition. *Maggie* offended traditionalists because of its subject matter. It is about a woman who becomes a prostitute—not a fit subject for literature doing the 1890s. It is about slum dwellers—unfit objects of literary attention, many thought. Its style flouts traditional conceptions of what literary style is or can be. Many found it morally and aesthetically offensive. *The Black Riders* was objectionable to some because of its religious and philosophical stance and because of its nontraditional style. It calls into question the traditional conception of God and His relationship to humankind, suggesting that God is not the caring parent He has been pictured to be, and it does this in a most unusual manner. Its poetry is unlike most poetry of its time and before, featuring, as it does, neither rhyme nor regular meter, and its language when it is poetic tends to be archaic and in its archaism ironic. The more traditional critics hated his work and lambasted it; the more radical critics loved it and proclaimed its genius. Fortunately for American literature, the less traditional critics won the day, and it was generally agreed among reviewers that *The Red Badge* was a most remarkable work of originality and modernity.

The first two American reviews, both unsigned, appeared on 13 October in the *Philadelphia Press* and the *New York Press*. Both are generally positive reviews recommending the book rather highly, but the New York review is noteworthy because it sounds the prevailing notes to be heard among the reviews during the ensuing months at the end of 1895 and the beginning of 1896: it is original, a work of genius, and it possesses great power. The reviewer's coyness stems from the fact that it is one of the two initial reviews, and the reviewer is reticent about proclaiming the merits of such an unusual book by an unknown author: "One should be forever slow in charging an author with genius, but it must be confessed that *The Red Badge of Courage* is open to the suspicion of having greater power and originality than can be girdled by the name of talent." The concurrent *Philadelphia Press* review sounds the conservative note to be heard among the generally less receptive and positive reviews forthcoming in the next few months, choosing a passage from the novel to quote "not because it is a particularly fine one, but because it is fairly representative of the author's style and is singularly free from oaths and other horrors." The similarity between the *New York Press* review and the first of the British reviews (H. B. Marriott-Watson, *Pall Mall Gazette*, 26 November) is noteworthy. "Mr. Crane, we repeat, has written a remarkable book. His insight and power of realization amount to genius."

The very first American review, technically speaking, is a review not of the book as a novel but as a serial printed in the *Philadelphia Press* and appearing in that newspaper 3-8 December 1894, about a year prior to its publication as a book. The "review," in point of fact an editorial, constitutes the first, widespread acknowledgment of the significance of the book and its author in terms of American literature rather than in more parochial, limited terms. The *Press* views Crane not as a potential best-selling author but as a force in American literary history: "The indications are that upon that story [*The Red Badge*] is to be based the literary promise of a young man who it has seemed to those who have known him was likely to become one of the great men of American letters, and it is some satisfaction to know that the *Press* first of all papers in this country recognized the promise of extraordinary execution which seemed to be in this young man."

Among the most cautious of the early reviews is that of William Dean Howells, the dean of American letters at the time, appearing in the prestigious *Harper's Weekly* 26 October. The ambivalence revealed by Howells reflects the whole debate surrounding the reception of *The Red Badge*. He recognizes that the novel has a great deal to recommend it; yet he feels somewhat uncomfortable with it. He knows something unusual and praiseworthy is afoot, but he cannot give himself to it without extreme reservation. Note the ambivalence of tone in the opening paragraphs of Howells's review: "Of our own smaller fiction [note the condescension], I have been reading several books without finding a very fresh note except in *The Red Badge of Courage,* by Mr. Stephen Crane. He is the author of that story of New York tough life, *Maggie,* which I mentioned some time ago as so good [again note the character of the judgment rendered through tone] but so impossible of general acceptance because of our conventional limitations in respect of swearing, and some other traits of the common parlance." If we were to put all the American reviews together, we would find that they follow along the lines of Howells's ambivalence, either sharing it or supporting one pole or the other. The ambiguity of the national response had something to do with the claim made by the British litterateurs that they discovered Stephen Crane when he was rejected or ignored by his countrymen. The record shows this to be untrue insofar as it is clear that the majority of reviewers recognized an unusual and rare talent in Crane. There is, however, a significant difference between the American and English reviews, a difference that gives some basis in fact to the British claim. The crux of the matter probably lies in the character of the Howells review. Because Howells's review was probably the most significant one that the novel received in the U.S., it carried more weight than any other single review. The result is that its effect was to dampen the enthusiasm generated by the smaller and less prestigious reviews by lesser-known critics in less weighty publications.

It is clearly not true that the British reviewers "discovered" Stephen Crane; the American reviews, most of them earlier since the novel was first published in the United States, were positive and supportive. What is true, however, is that the British reviewers were more clear, explicit, and certain about who and what Stephen Crane was. We need only compare Howells's provincial categorization of Crane's work as belonging among "our own smaller fiction" with the great number of British estimates that classed his work as worthy of legitimate comparison with that of Tolstoi and Zola, as being, even, superior in significant respects to their work. The British reviewers were more sophisticated, and they tended to take Crane more seriously as an artist, to see him in more catholic terms than even the most receptive Americans. In some sense it seems that American critics did not have the confidence to believe that an American could do to and for literature what Crane did.

The novel did very well during its first year, and thereafter, it did well in comparison with most other novels. By the end of 1895 it had gone through fourteen printings in the United States. The greater enthusiasm of the British for Crane's novel caused it to go through six printings by the end of February 1896. It was reissued by Appleton in 1898 and again in 1900. During the years following Crane's death and leading up to World War I *The Red Badge* was the only work of Crane to be in print, but it, unlike all others of his works, has never been out of print since its first appearance as novel!

The reviews of the novel and the controversy that they sparked set the tone for the modern critical response to Crane (since 1950) insofar as they so early raised the kinds of interpretive questions that have preoccupied Crane's critics. The reviews—not only the favorable ones but the unfavorable ones as well—raised the thorny questions: Where does Crane fit within the literary tradition of America and Europe? How does he relate to his contemporaries as well as to his forebears? What are the sources of his style, and how can we talk about that style? What terms should we use? All the major themes, all the controversies and disagreements about the man and his work, have their genesis in the response of the citizens of Crane's world to his work, especially, most especially, to *The Red Badge*.

It was a good while, though, before the world of criticism caught up to the reviews, before criticism was inclined and able to delve into the questions raised by the first public response to Crane's novel. We lacked the understanding, the knowledge, the interest, the tools, the method, indeed, necessary to deal with the issues raised by Crane's work. Some fifty-odd years of preparation made it possible to accord *The Red Badge* (and Crane's writing in general) the level of serious treatment it deserved. The road was a long one, however, for only a very few years after Crane's best-known novel flashed upon the scene, his reputation had waned considerably. Because of his diminished stature, he was sorely in need of money during the last years of his short life, and though his work was being published, its proceeds did not nearly fulfill his financial needs.

In a 1912 letter Joseph Conrad marks the nadir of Crane's posthumous critical reputation: "Poor Crane was at one time 'puffed' but he was never properly appreciated. . . . mere literary excellence won't save a man's memory. . . . I hardly meet anyone now who knows or remembers anything of him. For the younger oncoming writers he simply does not exist."[1] Crane was not, however, forgotten for good. It might have taken the focus on war occasioned by America's entry into World War I to prompt memories of the country's war experiences and hence memories of Stephen Crane, for the publisher Appleton brought out *The Red Badge* again in 1917 and then reissued it three more times in that single year. Interest in Crane was thereby kept alive, an interest sustained, though perhaps by a thread, during the next decade.

It was not a focus on *The Red Badge* alone, however, that was responsible for the continued interest in Crane during the twenties. As it happened, the attention accorded him over the years resulted finally in a few of his works being acknowledged as masterpieces, *The Red Badge* chief among them. This attention is signaled by two major events in the history of the novel's critical reception: the publication of Thomas Beer's biography in 1923, *Stephen Crane: A Study in American Letters,* and Wilson Follett's edition of Crane's complete works in twelve volumes, *The Work of Stephen Crane* (1925–27). Beer's biography was not to be superseded for the next quarter of a century. The Follett edition of Crane's work was expensive and it contained many textual problems, yet its existence assured that most of

Crane's work was available for reading and study over the coming years until better texts could be prepared. Again, though *The Red Badge* does not specifically owe its critical reputation to these two seminal works, their publication was in large measure responsible for continued attention to Crane's writing.

A significant quantity of memoirs and other writings about Crane appeared in the 1920s, many of them by well-known critics and writers. Most of these were of a somewhat general nature; few of them focused on specific works. Each volume of the Follett edition of Crane's work was introduced by a well-known writer or critic of the time, and these sympathetic introductions, though none of them stands as a particularly insightful piece of criticism, probably served to enhance the sluggish growth of Crane's reputation. Some of these writers were Amy Lowell, Willa Cather, Sherwood Anderson, Joseph Hergesheimer, and Joseph Conrad.

Sporadic commentary on Crane continues through the thirties. Its amount is not overwhelming, but its budding character makes it in some ways different from that of the preceding decade, and it shows change. There seems, for example, to be a developing academic interest in Crane's work. Toward the end of the decade two seminal articles on possible sources of *The Red Badge of Courage* appear along with another on Crane's college education in a leading academic journal, *American Literature*. Several academic critics write on Crane, and that suggests that he is beginning to be accepted as a writer whose work merits the attention of professional scholars. In 1936 Hemingway in *The Green Hills of Africa* makes his famous comment on Crane: "The good writers are Henry James, Stephen Crane, and Mark Twain. That's not the order they're good in. There is no order for good writers."

The forties sees an intensification of the academic interest in Crane. The first doctoral dissertations were written during this time. Crane begins to be frequently anthologized, for example in the influential Cleanth Brooks and Robert Penn Warren's *An Approach to Literature* (1941). Hemingway includes *The Red Badge of Courage* in *Men at War: The Best War Stories of All Time* (1942), commenting in the introduction that the novel "is one of the finest books of our literature, and I include it entire because it is all as much of a piece as a great poem is." Alfred Kazin in his widely read volume on American literature *On Native Grounds* (1942) features Crane prominently. The work of Vincent Starrett and Ames W. Williams, *Stephen Crane: A Bibliography* (1948), sets the stage for the explosion of critical interest in Crane, and especially in *The Red Badge,* which took place in the fifties, thereby setting the stage for the study of the novel particularly and Crane's work as a whole.

Several things occurred in a relatively short time that were responsible for the critical focus on Crane's war novel. First of all, the early fifties saw the results of a shift in the focus of criticism that encouraged detailed analysis of single works of literature and even of parts of single works. (Until this time there are only about four articles, exclusive of reviews, that focus entirely upon a single work by Crane.) The important events leading up to the critical focus on *The Red Badge* were the publication of John Berryman's critical biography of Crane (1950), Robert W. Stallman's introduction to the Modern Library edition of *The Red Badge of Courage* (1951), which contains one of the earliest modern analyses of the novel, and the same critic's *Stephen Crane: An Omnibus* (1952). Many other events influenced critical attention to Crane's novel, but these were the main ones. Other significant critical works were Lars Ahnebrink's *The Beginning of Naturalism in American Fiction* (1950) because of its study of the relation of Crane to other writers, particularly European, and because it signals the beginning of international interest in Crane for the first time since the publication of *The Red Badge.* Chief among these early fifties publications is Stallman's *Omnibus.* Stallman's book made a cross section of Crane's work widely available, and it was probably through the *Omnibus* alone or through its abundant critical apparatus that most critics became engaged with Crane's fiction. Stallman's influence stemmed also from the great amount of controversy generated by his work. The 1950s saw the first articles of a critical nature published in major journals by Shroeder (1950) and Hart (1953), the latter's work on *The Red Badge* (see bibliography). Daniel Hoffman's *The Poetry of Stephen Crane* appeared in 1957 along with many other articles specifically on the war novel by such critics as Cox, Marcus, Solomon, and Weisberg. Criticism of the novel since the fifties has followed the paths charted then.

Several responsible editions of the novel have appeared, each of which has contributed to the growth of its critical reputation in one way or another. Chief among them have been the earliest modern one, the Rinehart edition edited by William M. Gibson, 1950, 1957, 1960; the Stallman editions, the *Omnibus* (mentioned above), the Signet edition (1960); the Joseph Katz facsimile edition, Charles E. Merrill (1969), and his Viking Portable *Stephen Crane* (1969); the Norton Critical Edition of *The Red Badge* edited by Bradley, Beatty, Long, and Pisor, 1976.

The critical response to *The Red Badge of Courage* has made clear that it is a major text of American literature. The first response to his work suggested that Crane's talent was a major one, but it took over fifty years of hundreds of readers reading and responding to his work before the testimony rendered in the most astute of the initial reviews received confirmation. Criticism over the past two or three decades has examined Crane's novel from psychological, sociological, philosophical, aesthetic, religious, and moral perspectives. In the foreseeable future this is not likely to change; that is, the criticism yet to be seems likely to seek to modify, affirm, or qualify what has gone before. Perhaps reevaluation of the novel is possible, but the history of the critical reception of *The Red Badge* suggests that its position as a classic of American literature is not likely to change significantly.

A Reading

4

A World of Conflict

The world of *The Red Badge of Courage* is one whose existence seems based on conflict. That is, it is not a world where conflict simply occurs; rather, it seems that conflict is necessary to the very operation of the world. Conflict makes things happen. The conflict that Crane describes in the novel and seems most interested in is conflict that threatens to erupt into violence as, indeed, it sometimes does. In *The Red Badge* and elsewhere in his fiction Crane dwells on fear, and that fear is most often the result of actual or potential conflict. We see this interest exhibited early in the novel, in its very first scene, where "a certain tall soldier" (11), upon his hasty return from washing his shirt, begins excitedly to tell the other soldiers what he has just heard about the impending movement into battle of their company. He assumes an air of pride as he speaks "pompously" of the group's future. "He adopted the important air of a herald in red and gold" (11). After he conveys his information, the soldiers break up into "small arguing groups" (12). "It's a lie! that's all it is—a thunderin' lie!" (12) a "loud" soldier exclaims. The bearer of the information and the "loud" soldier nearly come to blows. A spirited debate erupts among the soldiers as they engage in vigorous argument about whether the rumor is true.

A "youthful private," whom we later learn is Henry Fleming, reacts to the fracas around him by remaining silent and then retiring to his makeshift dwelling where he seeks the solace of isolation and escape from the conflict. He is worried, and his state of mind is partially revealed by what he sees as he enters: rifles (instruments of war) hang upon the wall; the sunlight *beats* upon the tent; a square of light is *shot* through the window onto the floor; the "flimsy chimney" makes "threats" to set the place on fire. We are told earlier that he seeks the shelter of his dwelling because "he wished to be alone with some new thoughts that had lately come to him" (13). That is perhaps the reason he gives himself, but it is not an entirely candid one. He wishes to escape the conflict among his fellows because it reminds him of the imminence of battle, of actual conflict with an opposing army, and this stirs in his unconscious mind a fear, a fear ultimately of the possibility of his own annihilation. I say "unconscious" because Crane's account of what is going through Henry's mind does not suggest that he is conscious of being afraid. The succession of ideas that proceeds through his head suggests that Henry is afraid; and later, as Henry fantasizes about the coming encounter, that unconscious fear finds its way to consciousness.

His thoughts wander from his first wanting to enlist, some time earlier, to his present situation, at the novel's beginning. His thinking finally leads him to consider the possibility that in a battle he might run. Before the present time he would not even have considered the question, "but now he felt compelled to give serious attention to it" (18). It is at this point that "a little panic fear grew in his mind." But had he not thought of this before? What lay behind Henry Fleming's burning need to enlist in the army, an action that will almost certainly bring him into direct and open conflict with an opposing army and perhaps bring about his death?

Henry does not have a realistic notion of what war is (as his thinking about it reveals). He believes, first of all, that it has to do with "heavy crowns and high castles." And he further believes it to be a thing of the past: "Secular and religious education had effaced the throat-grappling instinct, or else firm finance held in check the passions" (17). He also concludes that battles such as those described in the *Iliad* and the *Odyssey* represent conflicts that "will be no more." Yet Henry's fantasies have been shaped by his knowledge of fairy tales and mythology, and he is thus misled about what war will actually be like. He also wants the glory that he associates with war. Therefore, when he finds himself facing the prospect of engaging in battle and wondering whether he will flee when the time arrives, he is facing a problem altogether new, for he had not previously imagined the difficulty he finds himself in. Before he enlisted he had not thought that he might be fearful, and as he imagined it, war carried no threats to life or other significant dangers.

Henry's motives for putting himself in a position to face the conflicts occasioned by war are probably not as apparent to him as they are to the reader of *The Red Badge*. The clues to his most basic motivations are revealed in the first chapter, where we learn that Henry's understanding of what war is has been gleaned from his knowledge of fairy tales and mythology. He sees himself as being not unlike the heroes who appear in the tales he has read or heard during his life. For this reason he is disappointed when his mother fails to deliver the parting injunction to young Greek warriors on their departure for war, that he must return "with his shield or upon it," that it is better to be killed than undergo the infamy of losing one's shield. That expectation on Henry's part is both innocent and naive, especially in view of the fact that Henry will have no shield. It tells us, however, how he views himself and his situation.

In seeing his circumstance as that of the hero of myth and fairy tale, Henry half-consciously believes that he is about to embark upon an adventure during which he will encounter hostile forces that he, by strength of will and arm, will overcome and hence be transformed into a hero. Throughout the narrative Henry draws comparisons indicating that he thinks of himself as such a hero. The opposing army is a "red and green monster," composed of "redoubtable dragons" who threaten to gobble him up. He sees himself as a "knight," and toward the end of the novel the enemy's flag becomes "a craved treasure of mythology" (127) and his own "a goddess, radiant, that bended its form with an imperious gesture to him" (110). In one sense the comparisons reveal Henry's innocence and naïveté; in another they are apt and fit comparisons, for central to all such tales as those Henry refers to and central to his wartime situation are the elements of conflict and danger. Henry's own saga begins prior to his joining the army. That is why he tells us something about his life at home before he leaves there.

It is not inconsequential that Henry's father had died and that he is forbidden to enlist and leave home by his mother when he initially seeks her permission. He is not conscious of it, but one of his purposes in leaving home to join the army is to seek the strength of character and consciousness necessary to displace the authority of his mother with his own. The conflict between Henry and his mother has its surface meaning and its submerged meaning. On the surface the conflict is about whether Henry should remain at home where he is safe and where he can help his mother take care of the farm. Underneath, something far more complex is taking place. The conflict is a battle for authority though neither knows that consciously. Henry has reached an age far enough advanced, as he sees things, to feel the urge to take control of his life, assuming authority for it and responsibility. In order to do so he must subvert or otherwise undermine the established parental authority centered, since the death of his father, in his mother. His first step toward autonomy is in his defiance of his mother's injunction when he tells her he is going to join the army: "Henry, don't you be a fool" (14).

His defiance of her imperative does not deter her from fulfilling her role, as she sees it, as an authority figure. In an attempt to maintain her authoritative role in his life she tells him how he should conduct his life, and in order to assure the maintenance of her position she emphasizes her role as mother, as sustainer and protector. He wishes a clean break between them ("He had prepared certain sentences which he thought could be used with touching effect. But her words destroyed his plans. She had doggedly peeled potatoes [thereby sustaining her role as nourisher—'doggedly'] and addressed him as follows . . ." 15), but she will not allow it, and this is the source of his annoyance. Her words tell him that he is above all not to attempt to assume authority, that he is to remain in his place. "Yer just one little feller amongst a hull lot of others, and yeh've got keep quiet an' do what they tell yeh. I know how you are, Henry" (15). In instructing him about how he should behave she advances a strong effort to convince him that he should remain dependent and in a childlike relation to her. "I've knet yeh eight pair of socks, Henry, and I've put in all yer best shirts, because I want my boy to be jest as warm and comf'able as anybody in the army. Whenever they get holes in 'em, I want yeh to send 'em rightaway back to me, so's I kin dern 'em" (15).

Her attempt to dominate, to prevail in the underlying conflict between Henry and herself, is everywhere apparent through the course of their interaction. After she tells Henry about the socks, a practical reminder of his need for her, she immediately follows that with an injunction regarding his conduct. The implication of the juxtaposition of the two statements is that they are related. The logic goes that the price of your needing me is my resulting prerogative to dictate your conduct. Because she has knit him eight pairs of socks (a traditionally female and motherly task), she may likewise advise him about how to conduct his life: "An' allus be careful an' choose yer comp'ny." She warns Henry that there will be plenty of men who will want to teach him bad things such as drinking and swearing (again she

23

assumes that she has the authority to define what is good and what bad). She goes so far finally as to attempt to insinuate herself into Henry's consciousness when she says, attempting to assure herself that she is his conscience—hence, according to Freud, the voice of his father—"I don't want yeh to ever do anything, Henry, that yeh would be 'shamed to let me know about. Jest think as if I was a-watchin yeh" (15). At this point, recognizing that she as mother does not by tradition exercise the authority of the male parent, she invokes the name of Henry's father in order to buttress her authority: "Yeh must allus remember yer father, too, child, an' remember he never drunk a drop of licker in his life, and seldom swore a cross oath" (15). Her concluding words during this scene are intended to reinforce her intention to overcome Henry in the conflict: "Watch out, and be a good boy." Henry's intention during this time is to stop being the "boy" that his mother encourages and to start being a man, an adult. Her moral injunction that he should be a "good boy" is sugarcoated with her expression of his assumed need for her as a mother: "I've put a cup of blackberry jam with yer bundle, because I know yeh like it above all things" (16). She attempts to assert her authority through associating her orders regarding his moral direction with his emotional wants and needs.

He, on the other hand, understands emotionally but not intellectually what is going on in his mother's mind. He knows on some level of consciousness what she is doing, but he has no conscious awareness of the nature of the transaction between them. Consequently his response to his mother's expostulation is entirely emotional, not intellectual nor consciously understood at all. He is impatient, but he does not know why. We know that he expected that his defiance of his mother's wishes would bring a clean break from her, but Crane knows that that is not the way separation from parents and establishment of individual autonomy occurs. Therefore, Henry bears her response "with an air of irritation," and "He departed feeling vague relief" (16).

The final upshot, however, is that when he leaves his mother finally, he feels "suddenly ashamed of his purpose" (16). How can he be in conflict with the mother of his final vision, not the mother who attempts to dominate him, to win out in conflict, but the mother who is the sustainer and the provider, who, "kneeling among potato parings" (potatoes peeled undoubtedly during most of his life to feed him), has "her brown face upraised . . . stained with tears . . . and her spare form quivering" (16)? His feeling "suddenly ashamed of his purposes" allows the formation of the basis of the remainder of the novel. Had he felt utterly comfortable about leaving his mother, there would have been no basis for the adventures of Henry Fleming. Hence the conflict that lies at the heart of Crane's story has its genesis in the relation between Henry Fleming and his parents, especially his maternal parent since she is the only one who exists in the novel. In his attempt to become an individual, to separate himself from his mother and to assume the prerogatives of adulthood, Henry feels the need to prove himself. Is it any wonder, then, that when he ruminates about what will be the character of his performance in battle, and especially when he has doubts about whether he will do well, he should think about being back home where he was not beset by such monstrous threats as those posed by the imminent conflict with a seemingly impervious adversary?

Nobody disagrees that there is a good deal of conflict in Crane's novel; many, however, disagree about the resolution of that conflict and even about the nature of it.[2] Some feel that the tensions generated by Henry's personality and situation are resolved by the end of the novel. Others feel they are not resolved at all, but that Henry Fleming is in the same condition at the end of the novel that he was in at the beginning, that he has not solved nor resolved anything. Some feel that Henry is expressing his reactions to growing up, to becoming an adult; others feel that he is attempting to understand the very nature of the universe; others that he is doing both. Still others feel that he is doing neither but groping his way blindly and ignorantly through life because he adheres to traditional patterns of belief and action and is therefore bound to follow such a path. Let us explore what permits such a diversity of readings, none of which, though they are contradictory, is not without some support in the novel. No one of them can be dismissed out of hand.

Without attempting to resolve the question fully at this time we will broach the question of the novel's resolution of Henry's chief conflict—at least as it may be defined by one perspective on the book. Is *The Red Badge* the traditional story of the young man who leaves home, prompted toward psychological and economic autonomy, who then overcomes adversity, finds his way in the world, and settles into life on the verge of adult life and success ("happily ever after" the phrase is)? There are many, many elements of the novel that would encourage this reading. First of all, this is the way Henry seems to interpret his experience. He would be the first to agree that his is the traditional circumstance. His likening of his lot to that of the traditional hero of myth and fairy tale renders his opinion of what he faces, of how things are with him. If we compare Henry at the beginning of the novel with Henry at the end, it is clear that he feels he has changed, that he is not the same person he was before his experience of war. We are told on the final page of the novel, "He felt a quiet manhood, nonassertive but of sturdy and strong blood. He knew that he would no more quail before his guides wherever they should point. He had been to touch the great death, and found that, after all, it was but the great death. He was a man" (134).

We have seen Henry change from a fearful and trepidatious young man. At the beginning of the novel he was entirely uncertain of himself, unsure of whether he would be able to stand his ground in a battle. We saw him, indeed, run during his second encounter with the enemy, only to discover that he was one among a very few who cowered during seeming adversity and defeat. We saw him undergo a good many experiences that seemed to cause him to grow into a seasoned veteran, one who eventually was able to risk undaunted the possibility of his own annihilation, and to function fully and consciously without fear. We saw him grow in sensitivity and knowledge. Whereas the focus of his mind is initially inward and on his own interests, concerns, fears, and needs, he later is seemingly able to broaden his purview and thus to get beyond the limits of his own psychic universe. It would seem, as a matter of fact, that he not only is able eventually to relate to others but also to expand his vision to include the universe at large. This reading is further buttressed by its relation to tradition. This is the story that we *want* to read, the story that is like most stories we have known. It is a positive story; one which tells us that what we know and believe is right; one which does not threaten our received notions of truth and reality. It is the story, in broadest terms, of the individual beset with difficulties who by chance, fate, or exercise of will overcomes those difficulties and thus ends in a better state than that in which he began.

We also believe we know the causes accounting for Henry's transformation. We know that he feels ashamed after he has run from battle and that he feels he must somehow make amends. He does not want to appear cowardly to his friends or to any of the other soldiers. He fears that others will discover he has not been wounded and will wonder why he is with a group of wounded soldiers moving toward the rear. He is thus motivated at least to appear as though he is courageous, to conceal the fact that he ran during the battle.

Henry's character undergoes quite specific development during the course of the narrative. During his first encounter with the enemy he holds his position, but it is clear that he is not entirely conscious of what he is about. He finds himself "working at his weapon like an automatic affair." In relation to his comrades, "He was welded into a common personality . . . he could not flee no more than a little finger can commit a revolution from a hand" (41). It is also said that during this encounter he is in a "battle sleep." The implication is that Henry

27

has some way to go insofar as his goal is to stand and fight in a deliberate and conscious manner. Heroism, as Crane seems to define it, means not reacting in a wholly reflexive way, but acting consciously and willfully. The nature of the second encounter indicates that Henry has not achieved such a level of self-mastery and conscious control of his mind and body as to allow him to function as he wishes and needs to.

His preconceptions about experience and his too-great reliance on those around him to determine truth and actuality become his undoing in the second encounter. He has a framework (his notions about fairy tale and mythology) that predetermines what he sees, how he interprets what he sees before him. But this has to do with Crane's sense that individual perception of phenomena can take place only within a framework. Objective perception, perception outside of psychological, historical, sociological, and biological contexts, cannot occur. Hence he tells us how Henry is seeing things—he defines the perspective from which Henry views reality. That perspective is primarily emotional. Henry feels but does not think. He is a creature of emotion but not thought. His need to grow from one into the other is demonstrated in the second encounter with the enemy.

Prior to the beginning of the second encounter where he flees from battle Henry hears in the voices of his comrades only fear and doubt. "Why can't someone send us supports. . . . We ain't never going to stand this second banging" (46). When the firing begins, these very words recur to him, and he begins to allow his imagination to govern his perception as he exaggerates "the endurance, the skill, the valor of those who were coming" (47). Once again he reverts to his framework of knowledge about war gained from fairy tale or mythology: "To the youth it was an onslaught of redoubtable dragons. He became like the man who lost his legs at the approach of the red and green monster. . . . He seemed to shut his eyes and wait to be gobbled" (47).

We are told that during the first encounter Henry cannot flee just as a finger cannot leave a hand. That does not seem the case during the second encounter since he does in fact flee. The difference is that during the first encounter he acted as those around him did; since nobody around him fled, then neither did he. During the second encounter he again models himself on those around him. He does not look inward to discover what should be his mode of response. Instead, seeing a few soldiers run, he imagines that there is a wholesale rout, so "he, too, threw down his gun and fled" (47). The point is that his response during both encounters is the same; the difference is in the actions of those surrounding him.

The second encounter has the function of presenting the chief problem of the narrative. Henry's worst fear is realized when he flees from battle. Not only does he face the possibility of ridicule by his companions if his flight is discovered, but he has also let himself down in some extremely important, crucial ways. As he sees his problem, the issue is primarily that he has acted in an unmanly way, and his great concern is not the fact itself, but that others will know. The emphasis is on his desire for the approval of others because Henry is not in touch in a conscious manner with his unconscious concerns and motivations. We know they exist, for they impelled Henry to leave home despite his mother's wishes to the contrary. The problem presented by the events of the second encounter has to be resolved on two levels. Henry must achieve the strength to be self-reliant, for as long as he allows others around him to determine his responses, he cannot be the autonomous individual he needs to be. As long as he does what others around him do, he has simply shifted authority from parent to peer. Authority for his conduct should be internalized; it should lie within him. The "two" levels requiring resolution are in fact one in that they are two aspects of the same basic matter.

During the third encounter, after he has returned to his regiment with his "red badge," he is likewise not entirely conscious of what he is about. He fights well, however unconsciously: "The youth was not conscious that he was erect upon his feet. He did not know the direction of the ground" (99). And further, "He was so engrossed in his occupation that he was not aware of a lull." It is at this time that the lieutenant compliments Henry on his prowess as a fighter: "By heavens, if I had ten thousand wildcats like you I could tear the stomach out of this war in less'n a week!" (100). He is more consciously aware of his activities and in control than during the first encounter, yet his state is somnambulistic: "he was now what he called a hero. And he had not been aware of the process" (100).

The chief difference between Henry Fleming of the third encounter and the character as he was previously is that his chief response is not fear nor doubt, nor does he look to his companions for guidance. His chief emotion is rage, a tremendous anger directed toward the enemy. No longer does he see himself as the potential victim of monsters or dragons, nor does he direct his anger and frustrations at his officers. His assessment of his situation and circumstance is a more realistic one than ever before. He conceives himself not entirely as the aggressor but as one on the verge of being the aggressor: "It was not well to drive men into final corners; at those moments they could develop teeth and claws" (98). And further: "There was a sensation that he and his fellows, at bay, were pushing back, always pushing fierce onslaughts of creatures who were slippery" (98).

The encounter shows a more developed, mature, and consciously motivated Henry Fleming than before. Prior to its inception Henry and a comrade overhear two officers talking. The superior officer asks the other what troops he can spare in order to thwart the forthcoming charge of the enemy. Henry's regiment is named, and the superior officer says the charge will occur in five minutes, and he does not think that many of Henry's regiment will survive the charge. Henry knows at this point that the chances of his being killed are great, yet when he and his friend reveal to his comrades what they have overheard, they withhold the knowledge of the general's assessment of their chances of survival. Henry is well aware before the battle that he may be annihilated. He is not, however, deterred. "They [Henry and his friend] nodded a mute and unprotesting assent when a shaggy man near them said in a meek voice, 'We'll git swallowed'" (105). Note that the submerged comparison of the enemy to some large, devouring creature is exactly the comparison Henry had made earlier when he saw the enemy as a dragon or monster of some kind. If anything should immobilize him with fear five minutes before the encounter is to occur, *that* metaphor should, given the associations Henry has with it.

Other aspects of the fourth encounter suggest that Henry is undergoing significant change toward true maturity and that the novel is therefore traditional in its chief theme and its philosophical orientation. Though Henry showed in the previous engagement signs of a heightened and more controlled consciousness, he is even more highly aware of himself and his surroundings than ever before. Rather than even to consider the remote possibility of fleeing, he does the opposite: "He fixed his eye upon a distant and prominent clump of trees where he had concluded the enemy were to be met, and he ran toward it as toward a goal" (106). In the past, as already noted, Henry looks to those around him in order to determine his behavior. He is frightened because he sees his comrades killed or wounded. At this point, however, he seems unaffected, no longer fearing that the deaths of others necessarily presage his own demise. Earlier he might have quailed in the heat of battle. No longer. "The song of bullets was in the air and shells snarled among the treetops. One tumbled directly into the middle of a hurrying group and exploded in a crimson fury. There was an instant's spectacle of a man, almost over it, throwing up his hands to shield his eyes" (106). Henry is not paralyzed by seeing others wounded. "Other men, punched by bullets, fell in grotesque agonies. The regiment left a coherent trail of bodies" (106).

Henry's imagination no longer dictates to him reality; he not only sees things as they are, but his consciousness seems heightened as well. "It seemed to the youth that he saw everything. Each blade of the green grass was bold and clear. He thought that he was aware of every change in the thin, transparent vapor that floated idly in sheets. The brown or gray trunks of the trees showed each roughness of their surfaces" (106–7). Before this time his focus has been so tightly upon himself and his fear of dying that he could not possibly have been as objective as he is here. The clarity of Henry's vision surely suggests that he has grown, matured, and that the problems articulated earlier are nearly resolved.

Further evidence of Henry's growth during the progress of the narrative lies in his becoming the regiment's color-bearer. He is aggressively engaged in battle when he sees the color-bearer shot. As he and his friend wrest the flag from the dying man and he in turn pushes his friend away, thus becoming sole possessor of the flag, he again performs a conscious act that has the effect of placing him in danger. As color-bearer he is in the forefront of his regiment, unarmed, and a conspicuous target for enemy fire. And he is in such a situation not by fate or chance but because he chooses to be. "Each [both Henry and his friend] felt satisfied with the other's possession of it [the flag], but each felt bound to declare, by an offer to carry the emblem, his willingness to further risk himself" (111). Needless to say, Henry could not possibly have performed such a feat earlier. As he becomes more and more experienced, he seems increasingly in control of his bodily responses. At one point during the battle as Henry stands at the forefront of the regiment as flag-bearer, the enemy soldiers come so close that Henry sees the details of their dress and features. He studies them, yet holds his ground unmoved by the threat of being shot and killed. "They were so near that he could see their features. There was a recognition as he looked at the types of faces. Also he perceived with dim amazement that their uniforms were rather gay in effect, being light gray, accented with a brilliant-hued facing. Too, the clothes seemed new" (114). Again Crane emphasizes the degree to which Henry maintains conscious control of his responses.

Henry's actions in general during the fourth encounter support the idea that he has undergone meaningful growth through his experience of war. Initially he imagines himself as a victim, and, imagining such, he becomes victim, though more through his imagination than through any external force. Later, however, he becomes as color-bearer a leader, haranguing his fellow soldiers, even pushing them in an initially vain attempt to force them into action. Though his sense of himself as victim is not entirely dissipated (recall the image of the cornered animal above), it is significantly modified. "As he noted the vicious, wolflike temper of his comrades he had a sweet thought that if the enemy was about to swallow the regimental broom as a large prisoner, it could at least have the consolation of going down with bristles forward" (114–15). This image expresses the possibility of defeat, but not of victimization, as might be the case were the regimental broom to go down with bristles backward. And finally, the last line of the chapter describing the fourth encounter clearly indicates change on the part of Henry and his fellows: "And they were men" (115), thus implying that they have arrived at a state different from what they were in in the past.

There is a fifth and final encounter, whose function is to show the pinnacle of Henry's development and maturation. He remains color-bearer, and demonstrates the same control and fearlessness as before. The bullets flying about do not present the same menace as before: "He knew that he thought of the bullets only as things that could prevent him from reaching the place of his endeavor" (126). And he feels consciously good that he is without fear: "There were subtle flashings of joy within him that thus should be his mind" (126). In the final encounter the enemy is defeated, the battle won—itself a signal of triumph. But not only is the battle won; the fight is the most desperate and determinedly fought of all. When Henry's regiment is ordered to charge an entrenched enemy, they must possess great courage, for the enemy troops are firing directly at them during the while. They have fixed their bayonets because they expect close, hand-to-hand combat. For the regiment, diminished in numbers as it has become, to win this encounter and the whole of their part of the battle, represents an astounding victory, not only for the group but especially for Henry. He, as color-bearer when they rush upon the foe, is in the greatest danger because he presents a clear target, the more so as the charge brings them ever closer to the enemy until they are finally face to face as "the space between dwindled to an insignificant distance." Henry has never been in greater danger, but he braves it intrepidly and with poise.

Henry's own view of himself at the end of the novel is clearly that he has undergone a significant change for the better, that he has matured. In the terms he chooses to describe what has happened to him, he has become a man. The narrative concludes with his thinking back over his recent past and attempting to understand and assess it. His comrades feel that he has performed commendably, which suggests an external basis for judging that he sees things as they are: "He recalled with a thrill of joy the respectful comments of his fellows upon his conduct" (131).

He feels that he can be proud of his "public deeds," but his private deeds, running from battle and then deserting "the tattered man," are hardly worthy of praise. The two are related because his reason for deserting "the tattered man" who is actually badly wounded when Henry is not is that his probing questions are threatening to Henry who is terrified lest it be known he fled from battle. Henry seems to feel more guilty about deserting "the tattered man," whose own impulse is to be helpful and friendly despite his severe wounds, than he feels about running from battle. Perhaps that is because he has redeemed himself of the one "sin"—so-called—by achieving the capacity to perform courageously. The other sin perhaps cannot be so easily atoned for since it can hardly be undone or made right in the sense that Henry can correct whatever flaw or fault prompted him to run from battle. In any case he agonizes over the deed and its memory is reproachful suggesting that he possesses a quality of character sufficiently self-critical to indicate to him that his act was a shameful one.

We have reviewed the evidence in Crane's novel that allows it to be read as a novel in which the central character through undergoing various trials achieves maturity and autonomy. Whereas we have focused only on the major evidence (e.g., we did not deal with the implications of the death of Jim Conklin or of the forest chapel scene) that shows the novel to be about growth and maturity, there is a convincing case to be made for interpreting the novel as what is called a traditional novel. There is also a very strong case for interpreting it as nontraditional, as a novel in which there is no positive progress on the main character's part at all, though he mistakenly thinks there is. He is therefore simply deluded as are those readers, from the perspective of the advocate of the nontraditional novel, who see Henry as growing and developing toward some desirable and worthy end. That is to say, Crane has written the novel, the nontraditional advocate would argue, in such a way as to insinuate that the reader who is as naive as Henry will of course interpret Henry's experiences as naively as Henry did. The more sophisticated reader will see beyond the narrow and limited vision of Henry Fleming, will see things in his experience that Henry never knew existed nor, given the limitations of his perspective, could he ever have known to exist. Let us see what happens if we look at the novel from this vantage point.

That the novel ends as it begins suggests circularity, and circularity suggests lack of forward movement, progress. The similarities between the novel's end and beginning are by no means conclusive evidence that Henry has not grown or matured. It is only partial evidence and must be seen in the context of other evidence. It is significant that in the opening paragraph Crane writes, "It [the army] cast its eyes upon the roads, which were growing from long troughs of liquid mud to proper thoroughfares" (11); and in the penultimate paragraph (effectively the final paragraph since the final paragraph consists of one brief declarative sentence) he should write, "The procession of weary soldiers became a bedraggled train, despondent and muttering, marching with churning effort in a trough of liquid brown mud under a low, wretched sky" (134). At the novel's end as at its beginning the soldiers are engaged in the same argument, almost literally the same argument, about troop movements. At the beginning the tall soldier reports the rumor he has heard: "We're goin' 'way up the river, cut across, an' come in behint 'em" (11). At the end an unidentified soldier speaks: "We're goin' down here aways, swing aroun', an' come in behint 'em" (133). One might infer that Henry is at the end in the same place he was at the beginning; the only difference is his subjective sense that something significant has changed.

How are we to read the two final paragraphs of the novel? In actuality, Henry is sloshing through rain and mud, and the sky is "wretched." His imagination is in quite another place as "he turned now with a lover's thirst to images of tranquil skies, fresh meadows, and cool brooks—an existence of soft and eternal peace" (134). Is Henry seeing things as they truly are? What kind of existence does he envision? What is "soft and eternal peace"? The war is not over, and even if it was and Henry was going home, what would such a thing mean? The final sentence is equally puzzling: "Over the river a golden ray of sun came through the hosts of leaden rain clouds" (134). Just what does that mean? It cannot mean that nature predicts anything positive for Henry because he (and we as readers) must certainly have learned by now that nature has no messages for

36

people. If he thinks so, if he thinks that "golden ray of sun" has anything to do with him, then he is surely deluded. And if he is deluded about the meaning of the sun, then may he not likewise be deluded about the meaning of the experience he has undergone?

5

Irony

The heavily ironic tone of *The Red Badge of Courage* may prompt one to read the novel as ironic throughout. The irony begins in the second paragraph where we are told: "Once a certain tall soldier developed virtues and went resolutely to wash a shirt. He came flying back . . . with a tale he had heard from a reliable friend, who had heard it from . . . who had heard it from. . . . He adopted the important air of a herald in red and gold" (11). The irony results from exaggeration and inversion. Cleanliness is good, but it has nothing to do with virtue or morality; "resolute" carries too much of the connotations of seriousness and high purpose to be attached to such a commonplace activity as washing a shirt. The implications surrounding the sources of the "information" conveyed by the tall soldier tell us that it is clearly unreliable. His sense of his own importance because he has been the bearer of such misinformation is highly exaggerated and without any solid foundation. The important point is that none of the soldiers is able to distinguish between knowledge and opinion, between actuality and imagination. Crane's irony contributes toward producing that effect both at the beginning of the novel and at the end. The effect of juxta-posing the meaningless debate about the movements of the reg-iment with Henry's "serious" thinking about what has occurred in his life during the course of the narrative is to undercut the apparent meaning of Henry's ruminations. The implication is that he is no more able than his fellows to distinguish truth from illusion.

The irony directed against Henry, as most of it is, increases in its severity as the novel progresses. Toward the end it be-comes somewhat more mild and less frequent, but the problem is that it never disappears altogether, and we may find it difficult to tell when we are to interpret Henry's thoughts ironically and when we are to take them in a straightforward manner. The irony contained in the passages describing his taking leave of his schoolmates is a mild and gentle irony, but it is no less ironic: "There was another and darker girl whom he had gazed at steadfastly, and he thought she grew demure and sad at sight of his blue and brass. As he had walked down the path between the rows of oaks, he had turned his head and detected her at a window watching his departure. As he perceived her, she had immediately begun to stare up through the high tree branches at the sky" (16). What Crane wishes to convey here is something of the extent to which Henry is self-centered and is inclined to interpret his experience in terms of his needs at any given time. Hence we cannot be sure that what Henry sees is actually there; at least, we cannot be sure that he reads the world correctly. Crane does not say, as he well might have, that the girl did in fact grow demure; rather, he says that Henry "thought" she did. Henry wants to believe that the "dark" girl is attracted to him so he understands her behavior as reflecting that. The question is how can we know when Henry is seeing things truly and how can we know when he is not? The phrase "as he perceived her" means two things: at the moment or time he perceived her, and the manner in which or *how* he perceived her, the latter mean-ing suggesting the subjective nature of Henry's interpretation of his experience. In any case it is apparent that Henry is seeing himself in a way different from the way Crane is seeing him. Such irony is indeed gentle irony.

As the narrative proceeds, the irony directed against Henry becomes heavier and more critical of his perception of himself. Prior to the first engagement, when Henry's regiment moves about from place to place and it seems they will likely see action soon, Henry feels enclosed by his regiment, as though "in a moving box." His thoughts at that point are patently untrue: "As he perceived this fact it occurred to him that he had never wished to come to the war. He had not enlisted of his free will. He had been dragged by the merciless government. And now they were taking him out to be slaughtered" (30). Such irony has a distancing effect in that it diminishes the sympathy a reader feels for Henry. Perhaps that is Crane's intention, especially if he was writing from the perspective presently under discussion. If he intends Henry to be the self-deluded hero and not the traditional one, then we might expect that there exists some disaffection between Crane and his hero and that the feeling would be communicated to the reader.

After the second encounter, the one during which Henry runs, the irony becomes more and more harsh, and there is no doubt that Henry is deluding himself entirely and in ways not the least bit subtle: "He had fled, he told himself, because annihilation approached. He had done a good part in saving himself, who was a little piece of the army. He had considered the time, he said, to be one in which it was the duty of every little piece to rescue itself if possible" (51). Again and again he attempts to justify his actions in fleeing, and his reasoning becomes more and more confused and clouded. "He had been overturned and crushed by their [his comrades'] lack of sense in holding the position, when intelligent deliberation would have convinced them that it was impossible. He, the enlightened man who looks afar in the dark, had fled because of his superior perceptions and knowledge" (51–52). At this point in the narrative—here Henry has just learned that the line held, that his regiment was not routed—the irony is crushing. Crane seems entirely out of sympathy with Henry, even to the point of being scornful in tone. The irony at this point remains consistently heavy: "He was trodden beneath the feet of an iron injustice. He had proceeded with wisdom and from the most righteous motives under heaven's blue only to be frustrated by hateful circumstances" (52).

Another kind of irony, dramatic irony, occurs initially when Henry meets the tattered man who assumes Henry to have been wounded in battle as are all the men in the procession headed rearward which Henry joins. We of course know that Henry has not been wounded at all. The interaction between them is marked by Henry's extreme fear that it will be discovered that he is not wounded and that it will be believed that he, since he has no reason to be away from his regiment, has either fled from the battlefield or deserted: "Because of the tattered soldier's question he now felt that his shame could be viewed. He was continually casting sidelong glances to see if the men were contemplating the letters of guilt he felt burned into his brow" (59). The disparity between what we as readers know and what those who surround Henry in the world of the novel know is sustained from the time of the occurrence of Henry's flight to the end of the novel.

The effect of Henry's pretense is to raise the question of the integrity of his character, for his greatest concern is not that he abandoned his comrades and acted in a cowardly way but that it will be *discovered* that he did. Never when he is alone does he feel shame or guilt except when he imagines he might be discovered by someone else. Such a consideration as this encourages the interpretation that no significant growth on Henry's part has taken place, for his fear of being discovered is not in any way resolved; he simply puts the fact of his cowardice out of his mind. He comes closest to feeling guilt after he abandons the wounded and ailing tattered man because of his fear of discovery. The desertion of the tattered man is the only act which Henry performs in the novel that he refers to as a "sin": "He gradually mustered force to put the sin at a distance" after he feels "a sudden suspicion that they [his comrades] were seeing his thoughts and scrutinizing each detail of the scene with the tattered soldier" (133). Earlier, thinking about how ignoble it was to leave the tattered man, he feels "a wretched chill of sweat . . . at the thought that he might be detected in the thing" (132). His running from battle is one kind of cowardice; his falseness and fear of discovery constitute another kind and one of equally significant magnitude.

The title of Crane's novel is itself ironic and offers evidence for one who would read the apparent change in Henry as merely illusory. When Henry is moving toward the rear with the procession of wounded soldiers and "he wished that he, too, had a wound, a red badge of courage," he means that he wishes he had received a wound in battle. A wound is a badge because it signifies something. It signifies that the possessor of the wound has exemplified courage by holding his place and not running during battle. So for Henry a "red badge of courage" would conceal the fact that he fled. It is a sign bespeaking his presence on the battlefield. The badge has this meaning to Henry. To others the red badge precludes raising the question as to whether Henry ran away. The wound therefore has one meaning for Henry and quite another for his fellow soldiers. For Henry and for the reader who knows that Henry received the wound from the rifle butt of a fleeing Union soldier (when Henry tried to stop him for questioning) it is not a badge of courage but a badge of shame and ignominy. That Crane thrusts the wound into extraordinary prominence by making it the title of the novel forces us to become aware of its ironic meaning. To those in the world of the novel who do not know any better, it is a "red badge of courage." When Henry returns to his regiment the treatment, the care, and solicitousness expended upon him are accorded to him because of the assumption that his wound was received in battle. We as readers know along with Henry what the badge *really* means.

The irony resulting from the discrepancy between the way he received his wound and the assumptions made by those who think he received it in battle is a long-sustained irony, for the secret is never revealed to Henry's comrades, and hence the irony exists through the conclusion of the novel. Not once does Henry see anything wrong with misrepresenting the cause of his wound. Not once does he show the slightest modicum of regret nor mortification for the fraud which he perpetuates by allowing others to infer that his wound was received in battle. He is without conscience as long as he feels his transgressions are undiscovered. The title of the novel remains an indictment of Henry's character insofar as that character is limited by his quite pragmatic sense of morality. Henry's greatest concern is that others think well of him—and he would have that at any price.

If we ferret out Henry's motivations during the course of the narrative, we would have to say that he is frequently driven by his sense of others' opinions of him and by his need to maintain the positive regard of those around him. At the narrative's beginning, when Henry wonders whether he will be, as he puts it, "a man of traditional courage," he is unable to discuss the matter with anyone else because he fears that he will be seen as cowardly. "He was afraid to make an open declaration of his concern, because he dreaded to place some unscrupulous confidant upon the high plane of the confessed from which elevation he could be derided" (21–22). Therefore he spends a great deal of effort concealing his chief concern and attempting to talk about it with others only in the most indirect ways.

There is a direct correlation between Henry's performance on the battlefield and his feeling that he is being observed and judged. When prior to the fourth encounter Henry overhears the conversation between the commander of his division and another officer, he learns that his regiment is regarded as the most expendable because "they fight like a lot 'a mule drivers"

(103). The epithet is seen by Henry as a stern, negative judgment, and the memory of it and his desire to efface it strongly motivate his actions during the forthcoming encounter. "A scowl of mortification and rage was upon his face. He had thought of a fine revenge upon the officer who had referred to him and his fellows as mule drivers. But he saw that it could not come to pass. His dreams had collapsed when the mule drivers, dwindling rapidly, had wavered and hesitated on the little clearing, and then had recoiled. And now the retreat of the mule drivers was a march of shame to him" (111–12). It is at this point that he becomes a leader, joining the lieutenant in rallying his comrades to greater effort. Prior to this scene Henry is indignant when the lieutenant grabs him by the arm, calls him "lunkhead," and screams at him to go forward, "as if he planned to drag the youth by the ear to the assault. . . . 'Come on yerself, then,' he [Henry] yelled. There was a bitter challenge in his voice" (109). Henry reacts as he does because he wants to correct the judgments of others who see him differently from the manner in which he wishes to be seen.

As the novel concludes, Crane makes clear to the reader the extent to which Henry is motivated by his desire to be thought well of by others and the degree to which he is conscious of being observed and judged by those around him. "Regarding his procession of memory he felt gleeful and unregretting, for in it his public deeds were paraded in great and shining prominence. Those performances which had been witnessed by his fellows marched now in wide purple and gold. . . . He recalled with a thrill of joy the respectful comments of his fellows upon his conduct" (131). It would thus seem that Henry is not so clearly "a man of traditional courage" unless traditional courage is something different from what most have thought it over the ages to be.

6

Heroism

One of the implications of the traditional view of heroism is that its chief motivation is internal, that it springs from resources within the psyche. It is generally believed that the relationship between courage and character is such that the two are not separable. Cowardice, most feel, stems from bad or weak character, and courage from strength of character. These are the assumptions with which we are likely to start reading *The Red Badge of Courage,* and they underlie the meaning of courage in the culture. Certainly the heroism as defined by implication in Western mythology and fairy tale is of this kind, and Henry Fleming's reference to fairy tale and mythology suggests that his view of the issue is not a different one. It would seem, however, that Crane in his novel calls these assumptions into question. The advocate of the nontraditional reading of the novel would argue that readers who see Henry as the traditional hero are not distinguishing between Henry's perspective and Crane's. Henry is the unknowing, unaware traditionalist, not Crane.

The implication of the foregoing is that Henry's sense of heroism is a false sense because, having its roots in myth and fairy tale, it does not derive from experience, but from knowledge transmitted through tradition. He need merely have the model of the courageous actor in order to emulate it. Little does he know that he absolutely cannot act in any way contrary to or unrelated to his personality and his own peculiar history. Heroism does not exist in a vacuum, apart from other aspects of personality. Hence Henry's conviction that heroism is defined by fairy tale and mythology is false, for it does not consider the social nor specifically psychological elements of heroism. Henry does not wish to be a hero for heroism's sake but because he does not want his fellows to regard him scornfully. On the contrary, he sorely desires their respect and high regard. Therefore his character is no better nor worse at the beginning of the novel than at the end because courage, at least the kind of courage brought under scrutiny by Crane's novel, has nothing to do with character. One need not be good in order not to flee from the line of battle. For that reason Henry's moral lapses—as when he conceals the origin of his wound and allows his comrades to infer its source—have no relation to his behavior in battle. His having run from battle can be concealed, for it is, though relevant in Henry's eyes, irrelevant in Crane's eyes and in the eyes of the careful reader.

Because he believes that there is a relation between courage and character, Henry's perception of himself is modified. He believes that a conflict exists between his heroism and his flight during the first encounter, for if the exhibition of courage is a manifestation of good character, then exhibition of cowardice manifests bad or weak character. By the same token he believes that his desertion of the tattered man may diminish the significance of his heroism if that act should become known. The text establishes clearly these associations. Immediately after the passage quoted above where Henry refers to his "public deeds" as "performances which . . . marched now in wide purple and gold," the narrator observes: "He saw that he was good. He recalled with a thrill of joy the respectful comments of his fellows upon his conduct" (131). Undoubtedly Henry feels he is good because he feels himself a hero and that feeling is confirmed by the responses of his comrades. By implication, the lines mean that Henry saw that he was good and they too saw that he was good. Immediately following the passage last quoted, Henry thinks of his flight: "Nevertheless, the ghost of his flight from the first engagement appeared to him and danced. . . . For a moment he blushed, and the light of his soul flickered with shame" (131–132). The very next line reads: "A specter of reproach came to him. There loomed the dogging memory of the tattered soldier." Clearly the association of these thoughts reveals a connection of some kind among them.

But how do we know how to read these lines? How do we know that Henry does not deserve credit for true guilt and remorse for past actions that are less than creditable? There is, first of all, the juxtaposition of ideas that shows that Henry is looking at the question of heroism from a rather unsophisticated perspective, that he thinks it some kind of fairy-tale affair. Beyond that Crane makes clear that the source of any sense of guilt or remorse is Henry's fear that his less-worthwhile deeds will be discovered by his comrades. Henry will go to any length not to be laughed at. There is also the clear irony of the final paragraphs pointed out above.

In addition, there is one line appearing in the novel's final chapter, quoted above for other purposes, whose ironic intent cannot be mistaken. The line is: "He saw that he was good." Recall in the account in the Old Testament of Genesis the line that recurs as one of a series of patterned refrains as the creation, step by step, is described: "And God saw that it was good." The rhythm and syntactical structure of the two sentences are nearly identical. Crane, the son of a deeply religious Methodist minister (who was raised as a strict Presbyterian), could not possibly have missed the parallel or created it by chance, especially since the creation myth was probably drilled into his head in Sunday school if not at home as well. Note that

Henry Fleming does not speak the sentence. Rather, the narrator attributes the sentiment to Henry. The implication is, then, that the line becomes a comment on Henry, a critical comment suggesting that Henry's pride at this point is so overweening that he would compare himself with God. If so, then we certainly may see him as deluded and his whole assessment of himself and his situation at this crucial juncture in the novel, a few paragraphs from the end, is called into question. This ironic thrust supports the view that though Henry is in a different place, he is not in a better place at the conclusion of the novel than he was at the beginning.

An enormous amount of further evidence suggests that Crane is not in sympathy with Henry during the final pages of the novel and that Henry is not seeing things as they are, but since this evidence is external evidence, i.e., excluded from the final version of the text as Crane presented it for publication, it does not have the same standing as evidence drawn from the text as he presented it to his publisher. The material referred to here comes from two manuscript versions of the novel, a shorter version, the first version of the novel as it was serialized in December 1894 for use by the Bacheller syndicate of newspapers, and the expanded version of that manuscript that became after further alteration the novel we know. Crane changed the manuscript version when it was in galley proof and produced the final text. Whether he changed his intentions between the preparation of the final manuscript and the version as printed in 1895 or whether changes in the text were made for some other reason, the expunged passages will give us some sense of how Crane was looking at his materials and will perhaps offer a clue as to how to read the text as it finally emerged.

The textual changes were in general made for different reasons. Some were made to sharpen the focus of the narrative, especially in cases where Crane's impressionistic style produced extended vagueness or misdirection of the reader's attention. Most of the names were deleted and the characters identified by attributes, for example, the "tall" soldier, the "loud" soldier, the "youth." A great deal of the change has to do with economy of style. The most significant changes, however, are extremely important changes that are intended to effect the very basic meaning of the novel; these are the ones with which we are primarily concerned. Interestingly enough, they appear in the final chapter where Crane attempts by careful manipulation of his words to handle his closure in such a way as to make the novel mean exactly what he intends it to mean. The modulations of style and meaning occurring there are most carefully wielded.

In the paragraph referred to above, where Henry thinks of himself as good, the final sentence, apparently expunged by Crane reads: "It was a little coronation" (131). The reference is to Henry's memory of the lieutenant's compliment to him after his performance during the third encounter: "By heavens, if I had ten thousand wild cats like you, I could tear the stomach outa this war in less'n a week!" (100). The "coronation" reference echoes an earlier passage in the text, also expunged by Crane, that clearly in its context indicates that Henry is not seeing things as they truly are. This passage occurs in chapter 15 after Henry has returned to his regiment and before the third engagement: "He returned to his old belief in the ultimate, astounding success of his life. . . . It was ordained because he was a fine creation. He saw plainly that he was the chosen of some gods. By fearful and wonderful roads he was to be led to a crown" (90–91). Clearly and severely ironic, this passage suggests that Henry is deluding himself. So does the "coronation" line in the final paragraphs of the text also suggest that Crane wants us to see Henry as deluded, especially as it stood before deletion, juxtaposed against "He saw that he was good."

Henry thinks back to his flight during the second encounter and in a heavily ironic passage he attempts to justify his past actions in obviously unintelligent and self-serving ways. For a moment after he recalls his flight, "his soul flickered with shame." The next line reads: "However, he presently procured an explanation and an apology" (132). This makes no literal sense, for there is no agency allowed for in the world of the novel to proffer such explanation or apology. The implication is that the universe explains his flight and apologizes to him for its necessity. Henry is being stringently ridiculed. The expunged passage continues: "He said those tempestuous movements [his flight] were of the wild mistakes and ravings of a novice who did not comprehend. He had been a mere man railing at a condition, but now he was out of it and could see that it had been very proper and just." The suffering occasioned by his fear of death and his fear of discovery are neither proper nor improper, neither just nor unjust; they simply are.

But Henry attempts at the novel's end, as he had earlier with fairy tale and mythology, to place his experience within a larger framework in order better to comprehend it. In this case he tries to see things in terms of a partially conceived conception of the relation of his experience to universal process. Thus: "It had been necessary for him to swallow swords that he might have a better throat for grapes" (132). There is nothing in the universe of the novel to account for such a necessity, and Henry is being foolish to account for his experience in such fashion. He simply seems more foolish, as the novel concludes, in his understanding: "Fate had in truth been kind to him; she had stabbed him with benign purpose and diligently cudgelled him for his own sake" (132)—again clearly ironic. When has anyone ever been "benignly" stabbed or "diligently cudgelled" out of kindness? The passage continues: "It was suddenly clear to him that he had been wrong not to kiss the knife and bow to the cudgel."

Crane seems here to intimate several things about Henry in this deleted passage. We see Henry structuring the universe as though the process is an exercise in the composition of fiction. He knows nothing about Fate yet in his egotism he is able to imagine that there is such a thing as Fate and that *she* (note the personalization) takes particular interest in his life. His thinking here probably derives from classical mythology just as his earlier thinking about war and heroism did. On another level, Crane is saying that even if the universe is structured as Henry implies, then he is still foolish to respond as he does. If there is an agency responsible for his fate, he is foolish indeed to see that agency as in any sense whatsoever benevolent. The irony is biting, and Henry seems the butt of sardonic humor. Is it possible to take the person seriously who so understands his experience when he sums it up as Henry does?

He is not through philosophizing, and the quality of the thought does not improve: "He was emerged from his struggles with a large sympathy for the machinery of the universe. With his new eyes he could see that the secret and open blows which were being dealt about the world with such heavenly lavishness were in truth blessings. It was a deity laying about him with the bludgeon of correction" (134). The implication here is that whatever misery, pain, and suffering are in the world exist for a purpose, for the purpose of correcting human error. They are blessings in disguise and should be welcomed. He feels in total sympathy with the processes of nature and the universe, and as such, "He could no more stand upon places high and false, and denounce the distant planets" (134). There is nothing obvious in his experience that would justify his conclusions. In fact, his experience should have shown him a quite different universe from that he creates. His belief seems also to express a religious fundamentalism, though we do not know its source. The notion that mankind are sinners and adversity is a sign of God's displeasure and intent to correct behavior and therefore a blessing is hardly enlightened theology. The deleted passage goes on: "He beheld that he was tiny but not inconsequent to the sun. In the spacewide whirl of events no grain like him would be lost" (134). What he learns is that "His [God's] eye is on the sparrow"; what he should have learned is that he is alone in an alien universe, entirely on his own.

Crane wrote a poem, which appeared in his volume of

poetry, *The Black Riders,* whose meaning expresses the exact opposite of Henry's thinking. The poem's epigraph, the occasion of the poem, is a biblical quotation:

> "And the sins of the fathers shall be visited upon the heads of the children, even unto the third and fourth generation of them that hate me."

> Well, then, I hate Thee, unrighteous picture;
> Wicked image, I hate thee;
> So, strike with Thy vengeance
> The heads of those little men
> Who come blindly.
> It will be a brave thing.

If we assume, without entering the labyrinth of critical theory that might legislate against it, that the poem (published the same year as *The Red Badge,* 1895) expresses ideas that Crane held when he wrote it, then that would suggest he uses the ideas professed by Henry to express his own thinking in an obverse way. In other words, we need merely turn Henry's thinking upside down in order to know what Crane thinks. Is, then, Henry "tiny but not inconsequent to the sun?" No. He is tiny but *in*consequent to the sun. "In the spacewide whirl of events" would a "grain like him . . . be lost?" Yes, a grain like him (and like all of us) would be lost.

The irony is on the verge of bitterness, and the final excised phrase is no less severe in its tone than the passages so far discussed. Let me put the expunged passage in its context, even though I have quoted the following passage before without the deleted passage, which is placed in brackets below: "He felt a quiet manhood, nonassertive but of sturdy and strong blood. He knew that he would no more quail before his guides wherever they should point. He had been to touch the great death, and found that, after all, it was but the great death [and was for others]. He was a man" (134). The phrase, "and was for others," is a *mighty* phrase, for it indicates that Henry's vision is so entirely warped that he has come to the point of believing that he cannot die. What is the effect of the irony of the brack-eted phrase on the sentence that follows? "He was a man" be-comes itself ironic and reflective of a deluded man. Without doubt, Henry is perceiving faultily; his psychological orienta-tion dictates entirely what he sees. He is incapable of the least objectivity because his sense of actuality is governed by an ide-alism whose force is so great as to prevent him from understand-ing his experience even on the most basic level.

Given the context we have just examined, the final line of the novel cannot but be ironic: "Over the river a golden ray of sun came through the hosts of leaden rain clouds," especially in view of the lines preceding it in the penultimate paragraph: "Yet the youth smiled, for he saw that the world was a world for him, though many discovered it to be made of oaths and walk-ing sticks." And of course, if the final line is ironic, then that means the novel has a completely different meaning than it has if the line is not.

Most of the material deleted by Crane from the novel has to do with controlling how we are seeing Henry Fleming. It would seem that Crane expunges for the most part material that is heavily ironic and makes Henry appear to be a fool or de-luded. He did not attempt to remove *all* such signals, but he wanted to alter the effect of the ironic substance on the reader's judgment of Henry. Had Crane left in the text all those deleted passages, the novel would be a different novel indeed. It would have been a confused text; as it is, however, Crane's sense of reality and actuality has left us a far more meaningful piece of work. The deleted material had to be removed in order to pre-vent our dismissing Henry out of hand. As it is, there are two major perspectives in the novel, the narrator's (Crane's—since there is no evidence that any disparity exists between the nar-rator's perspective and the author's) and Henry Fleming's. There is no question about which is the more authoritative. The narrator constantly judges Henry, from the moment we meet him until the close of the narration. Henry has no access to the narrator. He does not even know that the narrator exists. The narrator has a far more embracing consciousness than Henry, a far broader capacity to judge. A great deal of the difficulty surrounding the question of how to interpret the novel arises because the narrator's judgment of Henry is variable (not inconsistent), and that is one of the most realistic elements of the novel. Henry can be sympathetic, heroic, and sensitive; he nonetheless is quite capable of being selfish, stupid, and immeasurably cloddish.

In other words, we see Henry throughout the novel at his best and at his worst. We have discussed Henry at his best, at those times when the narrator is most sympathetic toward him and less censorious, and we have discussed him when he was not entirely good. We have yet to discuss him at his worst, when he is at his most dreadful, insensitive, and prideful moment. We can forgive Henry for running in the face of what he sees as imminent destruction, for the response is not conscious and intentional, but, rather, as he says, instinctive. It is less easy to forgive him for his handling of the letters of his friend, the loud soldier, Wilson (all one and the same person though the fact is obscured because he is referred to alternately by these appellations). Wilson gives the letters to Henry at the end of the third chapter in anticipation of his death during the forthcoming battle. It is an act of trust and faith. There is about the act an aura of self-pity and there exists something of a desire to have Henry commiserate with him in his fear and trembling. " 'It's my first and last battle, old boy,' said the latter, with intense gloom. He was quite pale, and his girlish lip was trembling" (35). When Henry returns to his regiment after his flight during the second encounter, the first person he meets is Wilson who is most solicitous toward him. Wilson gives him coffee, binds up his wound, acting toward him as a nurse. "Well, come, now . . . come on. I must put yeh to bed an' see that yeh git a good night's rest" (83). Finally he covers Henry with his own blankets, leaving himself no covers to sleep on or under. Henry objects. "The loud soldier snarled: 'Shet up an' go on t' sleep. Don't be makin' a fool 'a yerself,' he said severely." (83).

Crane delivers a strong judgment against Henry in having him decide to use the letters as a potential weapon against Wilson should he raise questions about Henry's whereabouts on the previous day after his running from battle. "He now rejoiced in the possession of a small weapon with which he could prostrate his comrade at the first signs of a cross-examination" (89). The same stringent irony leveled at Henry earlier is directed toward him again. Unlike the loud soldier, "He had performed his mistakes in the dark, so he was still a man. Indeed, when he remembered his fortunes of yesterday, and looked at them from a distance, he began to see something fine there. He had license to be pompous and veteranlike" (89). Henry uses the occasion of the letters and Wilson's shame at having to ask for them back as a means to make him feel superior to Wilson and to justify his atrocious conduct: "As he contemplated him, the youth felt his heart grow more strong and stout. He had never been compelled to blush in such manner for his acts; he was an individual of extraordinary virtues" (92). Chapter 15 concludes with Henry imagining that he is relating heroic tales of war to his mother and the young lady at the seminary who he believes (perhaps ironically because we cannot tell whether his perception of her reaction to him is true) has some romantic interest in him.

Between this chapter and the concluding paragraphs of the novel the irony slows somewhat and what there is is comparatively mild. This is an interesting phenomenon, for the question arises, what *is* happening here? Why does Crane no longer subject Henry to the same degree of ironic treatment, and why does he subject him any longer to ironic treatment at all? Let us first of all identify the irony occurring between the fifteenth chapter and the final paragraphs of the final chapter, the twenty-fourth, and then try to answer the other questions.

Henry, after he has found his way back to his regiment,

begins to imagine that he has not run from battle and that he may judge his superiors as one might who had been an active participant in the preceding day's battle events. The "sarcastic man," unknown to himself, reminds him of his true role in the events of late: "Mebbe yeh think yeh fit th' hull battle yestirday, Fleming" (95). The effect of the words is chastening: "The significance of the sarcastic man's words took from him all loud moods that would make him appear prominent. He became suddenly a modest person" (95). Thereafter Henry is not treated ironically until the conclusion of the next (the third) encounter with opposing troops.

His response after that encounter, during which he fights and is commended by the lieutenant ("If I had ten thousand wildcats like you . . ."), is markedly similar to his response after the very first encounter where he holds his ground. The manner of his fighting is the same too. In both instances he seems in a trancelike state ("The youth in his battle sleep heard this [the comments of another soldier] as one who dozes hears" (42) and he is enraged. During the first encounter "A burning roar filled his ears. Following this came a red rage. He developed the acute exasperation of a pestered animal, a well-meaning cow worried by dogs" (42). His response during the third encounter is quite the same. "He began to fume with rage and exasperation. . . . He had a wild hate for the relentless foe. . . . He was not going to be badgered of his life, like a kitten chased by boys, he said" (98). Many verbal parallels exist between the two scenes, e.g., "His impotency appeared to him, and made his rage into that of a driven beast" (42). This parallels a sentence describing the third encounter: "His knowledge of his inability to take vengeance for it [his feeling that he is taunted] made his rage into a dark and stormy specter" (98).

As the first encounter ends, Henry returns to consciousness as one waking from a deep sleep. "The youth awakened slowly. He came gradually back to a position from which he could regard himself. For moments he had been scrutinizing his person in a dazed way as if he had never before seen himself" (45). As he regards the meaning of his experience, he concludes: "So it was all over at last! The supreme trial had been passed. The red, formidable difficulties of war had been vanquished. He went into an ecstasy of self-satisfaction" (45). Henry's conclusion is retrospectively ironic because we know that during the next encounter, shortly after this moment, he flees.

At the end of the third encounter, again Henry considers the meaning of his battle experience and his conclusions are essentially the same as after the first. "These incidents made the youth ponder. It was revealed to him that he had been a barbarian, a beast. He had fought like a pagan who defends his religion. . . . He had been a tremendous figure no doubt. . . . He had overcome obstacles. . . . They had fallen like paper peaks and he was now what he called a hero. He had slept, and, awakening, found himself a knight. He lay and basked in the occasional stares of his comrades" (100).

The irony of the parallels between the earlier encounter and the later one is multifaceted. First of all, there is irony in the fact that Henry does not recognize that his responses in the two cases have been nearly identical, for if he did, he would not on the second occasion announce to himself that his problem is solved. He would have remembered that, after his first encounter when he believed "the difficulties of war have been vanquished," he fled. He therefore should recognize that the real test is in the next encounter, when he will see how he acts; whether he will run as in the encounter following the first occasion when he felt he was no longer afraid.

There is also irony in Henry's casting his inferences in the particular terms he chooses. That "he had slept and, awakening, found himself a knight" finds him using those terms of fairy tale and mythology that he had used when he first began thinking about himself in war. Those terms reflected his innocence and naïveté, and his use of them brings up the possibility that he is deceiving himself once again, not seeing things in a mature and reasonably objective way. We might also wonder whether he is seeing things as they are when he thinks, "He had been a tremendous figure, no doubt." We have seen him time and time again express a warped sense of self, and we may well wonder whether he is doing the same thing again.

It seems difficult to tell whether some passages after the fourth encounter and before the fifth should be read as ironic. How, for example, should the following passage be interpreted: "He [Henry] had had very little time previously in which to appreciate himself, so that there was now much satisfaction in quietly thinking of his own actions" (117). Again, before the fifth encounter, when a soldier reports to Henry and his friend that he has overheard the colonel and the lieutenant complimenting them on their courageousness in battle we are told: "They speedily forgot many things. The past held no pictures of error or disappointment. They were happy and their hearts swelled with grateful affection for the colonel and the youthful lieutenant" (120). Is it simply human nature that makes Henry forget that shortly before he was extremely irritated with both officers, or is it that his interpretation and judgment of the world alters with the wind?

Whether Crane intends these particular passages to be read ironically, the point remains the same. By his deletions (we have yet to consider his deletion of the whole of an original manuscript chapter 12) and his varying the existence or the intensity of the irony throughout, Crane intends to maintain control of the reader's response to the character of Henry Fleming. Irony serves well in Crane's attempt to modulate the reader's response, for he may withdraw the irony entirely, apply it heavily, or modulate its application through infinitely variable degrees between the two extremes. And this is what Crane, to the consternation of the reader who would have things one way or another, does. Throughout the text Henry appears more or less sympathetic, more or less deserving of blame or censure. This modulation of the reader's response is carefully and intentionally managed, largely through irony—and, as well, through editing of the irony when the negative or positive response elicited toward Henry seems too great or too little. The answer to the questions raised earlier, (why does Crane no longer subject Henry to the same degree of ironic treatment between the chapter in which he proposes to use Wilson's letters as emotional blackmail against him, and why does he subject him any longer to ironic treatment at all) is implicitly answered here. After Henry is at his most despicable moment, during the "letters" episode, he threatens to take over the text, to control the meaning and values expressed therein. It is not Henry alone who threatens to take over the text but a whole complex of values, the values contained within Henry's metaphors describing his own situation and condition. Tradition, the tradition that surrounds Henry on all sides, the iron laws of tradition, of which Henry thinks in chapter 3, also threatens Crane. Crane's counteraction is primarily through irony. That is why Henry is subjected to irony at the same time that he appears most sympathetic, when he seems most heroic and when his activity and behavior seem most acceptable. The irony is intended to counteract other textual movement. During the period when Henry is most positively presented, Crane must make sure that we do not misunderstand his intention. His irony is intended to insure that we interpret other things rightly. We need to see, for example, Henry's quite positive relation to Wilson, his friend, the loud soldier (all one and the same person, as pointed out before), in proper perspective. The irony allows this.

7

Human Relationships

With the possible exception of the tall soldier, Jim Conklin, Wilson is the only character other than Henry Fleming who has any significantly extended existence in Henry's world, at least that part of it described in the novel. Others, the tall soldier, the corporal, the lieutenant, exist, but they have little or no substance. Nor does Wilson at first. He is just "the loud soldier," a pasteboard figure whose role in the narrative is entirely a function of the degree to which his existence registers upon the consciousness of Henry Fleming. Jim Conklin registers early. He is the first character to be presented in the novel; he is the soldier who at the very beginning appears on the scene waving his just-washed shirt. Jim seems more commonsensical than Wilson. Wilson is simply a blowhard. Jim gives Henry reassuring advice regarding Henry's greatest concern, whether we will run from battle: "'Well,' said he profoundly, 'I've thought it might get too hot for Jim Conklin in some of them scrimmages, and if a whole lot of the boys started and run, why, I s'pose I'd start and run. And if I once started to run, I'd run like the devil, and no mistake. But if everybody was a-standing and a-fighting, why, I'd stand and fight'" (20). The advice is good, practical advice, psychologically sound, but not heroic advice. When Henry comes upon the mortally wounded Jim Conklin later, the significance to him is that he witnesses for the first time the death of someone in the army he knows. The effect is to bring the potential of his own annihilation closer to home. Though the impact of Jim on his sensibility is greater than the impact of Wilson, still he does not know Jim as well as he knows Wilson because his acquaintance with Wilson is more intimate and extended.

Wilson's relation with Henry parallels the most emotional relation Henry has in the novel. Wilson's relationship to Henry is not entirely like Henry's relation to his mother, but it is closer than any other relationship that Henry has. There is not the slightest hint of any other than ordinary relations between them, yet Wilson's care and concern for Henry are more motherly than the responses to him of anyone else in his environment. We have noted Wilson's motherly (nursely) concern for him when he returns to his regiment after receiving his "red badge" prior to the third encounter. Perhaps "motherly" is not the precise word. The point is not to name the relationship accurately so much as to indicate the nature of it. Obviously, men may act in a motherly fashion to each other without being unmanly. And that is the point here. Wilson has a genuine concern with the well-being of Henry, a concern born of his engagement with the question of how Henry is faring. After the third encounter, when Henry has appeared as a "war devil," Wilson "came staggering to him. There was some fright and dismay in his voice. 'Are yeh all right, Fleming? Do yeh feel all right? There ain't nothin' th' matter with yeh, Henry, is there?'" (100). The point is that for the first time since he left home someone has a clear and direct interest in his well-being.

His relation to Wilson may be regarded in a number of ways, as good or bad, as positive or negative. It is good in that it brings Henry out of himself and into relation with another human, which forces Henry to see things in a more objective

way. Wilson acts as a check on reality and as a model of conduct. One of the reasons that Henry is able to go unflinchingly
into the fourth engagement is that Wilson is with him and they
are mutually supportive. They are both aware, as pointed out
above, that their chances of getting back, insofar as they know,
are slim. They look to each other for support and they find it in
each other's faces: "The youth, turning, shot a quick inquiring
glance at his friend, the latter returned to him the same manner
of look" (105). They are the only ones who know of the likeli-
hood that they will not get back. Their decision to go forward,
to participate despite their knowledge, is clearly a mutual and
not individual decision. They respond as they do because they
are two and not one: "They saw no hesitation in each other's
faces . . ." (105). What is to be noted is the sharp contrast between Henry's situation here and at the beginning of the novel
where he is so entirely alone: "The youth, considering himself
as separated from the others, was saddened by the blithe and
merry speeches that went from rank to rank" (24). "The youth
kept from intercourse with his companions as much as circumstances would allow him" (25). Initially he can hardly communicate with anyone about the most basic matters regarding what
will happen to him in battle. These two look to each other for
confirmation, support, and encouragement, and they find it.

Henry at first probably needs more from Wilson than con-
versely, for Wilson is the more experienced warrior and has
more significantly matured. But their relative positions in regard
to courage, their positions in regard to each other, are not static.
There is a dynamic in their relation; it changes and develops.
For example, Wilson at first has no name—he is simply "the
loud soldier" until the thirteenth chapter, after Henry has received his wound and been led back to his regiment. Wilson is
doing guard duty when Henry returns: "His *friend* had stepped
forward quickly [my emphasis]" (80). Thereafter he is referred
to as Henry's or the youth's "friend." and never again is he "the
loud soldier." Obviously his loudness was indicative of his lack

of control of his responses, a general lack of maturity. We have noted Wilson's solicitous behavior toward Henry as he nurses the wound. Though Henry's insecurity and fear threaten to disrupt the relationship through the letters Wilson asked Henry to hold, he finally does not use them against him since Wilson does not threaten to unmask Henry's cowardice of the preceding day.

Before the third encounter Henry is rather nervous, and he expresses it through his incessant complaints that the regiment's being marched hither and yon simply shows that the officers in charge do not know what they are doing. The seasoned and matured "loud soldier" Wilson, no more the contentious and cantankerous adolescent he was before, reassures him as an older and more experienced person might comfort a younger one with a more volatile temperament: "The friend . . . interrupted his comrade with a voice of calm confidence. 'It'll turn out all right in th' end,' he said" (96).

The strength of the relation between Henry and Wilson is reflected in other ways as well; it is a subtle, developing relation. Recall that Henry has cast his notion of war's conflict in terms of fairy tale and mythology and that these terms mean more to him than any abstractions about experience possibly can. Up to this point he has over and over again understood his experience in terms of fairy tale and mythology. His most formidable opponents are not unlike those characters who appear in myth and fairy tale. There is extraordinary significance in his *sharing* the notion of annihilation with another. This designates a change in character, a change from isolation toward engagement with another. "We'll get swallowed," he hears from a "shaggy man" (105). This is the voicing of his worst fear as expressed time and time again when he sees his situation in mythic terms. His response is different here. His reaction to the potential of being swallowed is not his usual private, internal, subjective response. Instead, when they both hear the "We'll get swallowed," Wilson and Henry look at each other and without hesitation nod a "mute and unprotesting assent."

Is the myth-fairy tale allusion ironic? Yes, it is, insofar as the framework that the allusion supplies is an inadequate assessment of the existing situation. It is not ironic to the extent that it is a reasonable paradigm of Henry's situation. Eventually their roles are reversed; Henry becomes the more self-assured of the two, the stronger and more independent. We saw Wilson change from a "loud" soldier to a more circumspect, introspective, and thoughtful individual than he had been before: "The youth took note of a remarkable change in his comrade since those days of camp life upon the river bank. He seemed no more to be continually regarding the proportions of his personal prowess. He was not furious at small words that pricked his conceits. He was no more a loud young soldier" (86).

The implication of the text up to this point is that the relation between Henry and Wilson is necessary for Henry's growth (insofar as we can agree that some measure of growth has occurred). Wilson changed from "the loud soldier" during Henry's absence, and apparently he did so on his own. Though Henry needs Wilson's assistance initially, he eventually outgrows his dependence, and this is shown in the novel in several ways. After the color-bearer of the opposing army is shot and Henry and Wilson vie for possession of the flag, Henry finally is victorious in the struggle, friendly though it is, as he roughly pushes his friend away. They are equally desirous of carrying the flag and exposing themselves to danger, but it is significant that Henry fears no less than the matured Wilson the danger of thus exposing himself to enemy fire. The struggle and its outcome bespeak Henry's diminished emotional dependence on his friend, Wilson.

Before the fourth encounter, when it appears as though Henry's regiment may be defeated, Wilson comes to Henry in a mood not dissimilar from that he bore when he approached Henry with the packet of letters prior to the group's first encounter at the end of the third chapter. Wilson says to Henry that the first encounter is to be his first and final battle and that he has no chance of surviving. Henry does not quite know what to do at that time. When Wilson approaches him again with, "Well, Henry, I guess this is good-bye-john," Henry is not affected. He has on this occasion his own advice: "Oh, shut up, you damned fool!" (113). Earlier he might have been frightened by a comrade's fear, but not now. This little interaction also suggests that Henry is less needful of the emotional support offered by Wilson heretofore.

At the root of the relation between Henry and Wilson is Henry's fear of being laughed at. Easily stung by disapproval, especially sharp or widespread disapproval, Henry feels that Wilson is so greatly accepting that Henry need not fear that he will judge him. Henry sees himself in the soldier who attempts to steal a horse from a farmyard. The reactions of the regiment to the struggle between the pilferer and a farm girl are typical in that the soldiers seem to thrive on belittling, berating, or otherwise discrediting each other. "They jeered the piratical private, and called attention to various defects in his personal appearance" (25). Henry chooses to relate the incident because its effect on him is such as to remind him of the precarious situation he and his comrades are in. The slightest misstep may bring down upon one the disapprobation of everyone around. "There were crows and catcalls showered upon him when he retreated without the horse. The regiment rejoiced at his downfall." His comrades are ever on the ready to judge: more experienced soldiers call less experienced ones "fresh fish," officers refer to enlisted men as "mule drivers," or "mud slingers," "the lieutenant calls Henry "lunkhead." But he knows Wilson will not judge him, and for that reason he is admitted into the inner circle of Henry's trust, but no one else is.

8

Nature

Another source of aid in determining how to read *The Red Badge of Courage* is attention to one of its most important elements, an element clearly central to Crane's concerns, nature. The relation of humankind to nature is a frequent and prominent concern in Crane's fiction and poetry throughout his career, a phenomenon not entirely surprising if we recall the extent to which his nineteenth-century American literary forebears were engaged with that issue. Crane, however, saw nature in a completely different way from the way that Emerson and Thoreau perceived it on the one hand and Hawthorne and Melville on the other. For Emerson and Thoreau nature is an intermediary whose existence allows access to a higher level of reality, of being. Contemplation of nature allows the possibility of transcending the natural world and at once comprehending that which lies beyond. In the first section of his essay "Nature" Emerson speaks of the woods as "plantations of God" and says that "in the woods we return to reason and faith." He says further, in the essay, "an occult relation between man and the vegetable exists. . . . They nod to me, and I to them."

In the fiction of Hawthorne and Melville the implications of the relations between humankind and nature are not quite so straightforward and clear, at least in the sense of being wholly positive and unambiguous. We find in Hawthorne that nature has both a good and an evil dimension (as opposed to Emerson who finds no evil in nature). In *The Scarlet Letter* nature is represented in the opening scene by weeds, "burdock, pigweed, apple peru," representing its sinister side; and by the wild rose, representing its positive side, whose relation to the human events is such that it may show the condemned prisoner emerging from the prison that "the deep heart of Nature [Hawthorne's capitalization] could pity and be kind to him." The weeds named above and other "unsightly vegetation" find "something congenial in the soil that had so early borne the black flower of civilized society, a prison." So whether nature's relation to humankind is positive or negative, the possibility exists in Hawthorne's fiction that nature is responsive to human activity, that some relation exists between nature and morality. This is further borne out later when it is suggested that a scarlet A, the symbol Hester wears throughout the novel, appears in the midnight sky. Whether it is an illusion is never made clear, but in any case the *possibility* exists that the relation between humans and nature is such that the letter A with all its multilayered symbolic human meaning could be replicated in nature.

Likewise in Melville's *Moby-Dick* nature is ambiguously related to humankind. It is never entirely certain whether the whale's maiming of Ahab is the result of an intention on the part of the whale itself or fate, or whether it occurs because of chance. Another possibility is that deity itself has malevolent purposes and interferes in the operation of nature in such a way as to influence directly the affairs of humankind. It may well be that Ahab, were he able to accomplish his will to "strike through the mask" by killing the whale, would uncover a principle existing behind nature, nature being but a veil concealing some metaphysical reality. When Ahab considers the whale to be either "principle," deity, or "agent" of deity, he at one and the same time proposes the relation between God, nature, and humankind to be a close and intimate relation whether God exists in nature as the whale or whether God directs the course of action of the whale.

Hawthorne and Melville differ considerably from Emerson and Thoreau in their view of the relation between humankind and nature. Considered together, however, they point backward and forward in a developing trend in America whose course outlines a historical sense of that relation. The legacy of the Puritans of the seventeenth century and early eighteenth is reflected in Emerson's and Thoreau's transcendentalism though surely the Puritan divines Cotton Mather and Jonathan Edwards would have found transcendentalism heretical. Be that as it may, the Puritans "read" nature no less than did the transcendentalists, finding the glory of God and evidence of His existence manifested everywhere in nature, His creation. The only thing preventing them from "finding God in the bush," as Emerson did, was their orthodox theology which said that God and nature are separate. When the orthodoxy dies away, as it eventually did through the later eighteenth century, then transcendentalism becomes possible, its Puritan origins somewhat concealed but nonetheless apparent to the close observer.

Though Hawthorne and Melville call into question whether it is possible to "read" nature, whether the human mind is capable of the objectivity necessary to interpret what it perceives clearly and correctly, they nevertheless pose the possibility. Both writers seem keenly aware of human psychology in a way that Emerson and Thoreau were not. Both are aware of the role that personality, character, and circumstance play in perception; both are aware that two people observing the same phenomenon might well perceive it differently. Emerson seems on the whole to assume that we all see the same things, that the psychology of individuals is uniform. The implication is that *any* mind through contemplation of nature will find it possible to transcend nature. Hawthorne in his short story "Young Goodman Brown" makes it clear by precept and example (by the reader's perception of the very story itself) that perception is heavily dependent upon individual psychology. Melville makes the same point in the chapter titled "The Doubloon" in *Moby-Dick*. But neither stands entirely opposed to Emerson's thinking, insofar as it rests upon assumptions about the clarity and objectivity of thought and perception. Both seem not entirely convinced of the extent to which human objectivity is possible in that they do not deny in their fictional worlds the possibility of its existence.

Crane sees nature in an entirely different way, but a way that has its own history and grows out of the same tradition from which issued the responses to nature just discussed of earlier American writers. Unlike earlier writers and even most of his contemporaries, notably Mark Twain, Crane did not entertain the notion that any kind of sympathetic bond exists between humankind and nature. In fact, he writes in such a way as to suggest firm and direct opposition to such a view. He had some support in this perspective, though he was the first American writer to carry that view into literature. He was the first American writer to write from the perspective that the human mind, consciousness, distances humans from nature. This is first apparent in Crane's first novel *Maggie: A Girl of the Streets* where the narrator's voice differs so considerably from the voices of the characters because they lack the degree of consciousness that gives the narrator the capacity to tell the story. That same distance between narrator and character prevails in *The Red Badge of Courage*, the tone of voice being a measure of the degree of consciousness separating the narrator from Henry Fleming.

For Crane neither the view of Emerson and Thoreau that nature is a manifestation of God and that God is even immanent in nature nor that, as Hawthorne and Melville suggest, nature *may* reflect God or contain Him (and thus their ambivalence on this issue), is tenable. Crane has been influenced by Charles Darwin and in his thinking has carried the implications of Darwinism to their logical conclusion. He was driven to do this because Darwinist thought conflicted with all that his Christian, Methodist background had taught him about the origins and meaning of the universe. (Many, many others struggled with this problem after Darwin's theory became widely known.) The Bible had told him in Genesis that God created the universe, the world particularly, and nature in the span of six days. He created man and woman in his own image and breathed into them the breath of life. Darwin told a quite different story.

Darwin began to believe, as the evidence grew, that species of living things are not fixed and immutable as Genesis implies. That is, Genesis suggests that God created all living species of life at one time and they remained unchanged from that time. Darwin's evidence indicated to him that species change and develop over time. Fossil remains indicated that existing species had previously existed in prior forms. Darwin yet had questions to answer, for he did not initially understand the mechanism driving change in species, nor did he at first know the amount of time that had been involved in the development of species to their then-current state because he, along with nearly everyone else, did not know the age of the earth. Calculated from biblical evidence, the age of the earth was thought to be about six thousand years. Such a proposition can not begin to accommodate the principle of evolution. Charles Lyell, whose *Principles of Geology* Darwin began reading when he started the voyage of exploration around the world on H. M. S. *Beagle*, said that the earth was many millions of years old, and that fact alone allowed the time necessary for the kinds of mutations in species that Darwin was later to postulate; it allowed the concept of evolutionary time. The principle of natural selection triggered by the concept of the survival of the fittest was fit enough explanation of how change occurred. The *fittest* organism is that best adapted to survive in its environment; others less well equipped to survive are snuffed out over periods of time, and those characteristics responsible for promoting survival are passed on until they prevail among the species. Such an account as this of the evolution of life on the planet does not require God; Crane knew that, accepted that, and explored the implications of it.

That Crane had Darwinism in mind, that such thought was a significant component of his frame of reference, is not a matter of speculation. It might well be inferred from external evidence such as that contained in *Maggie: A Girl of the Streets* where the conflict among individuals seems to mirror the conflict of animals in nature. Better, more direct external evidence, however, is that contained in the text as we have it of *The Red Badge,* an issue for later consideration. The strongest evidence of all is contained in the chapter discarded from the novel, the original chapter 12, where Henry, after witnessing the death of Jim Conklin, escaping from "the tattered soldier," and before receiving his "red badge" ruminates about his situation: "He made a little search for some thing upon which to concentrate the hate of his despair; he fumbled in his mangled intellect to find the Great Responsibility. He again hit upon nature. . . . He was of the unfit then. He did not come into the scheme of further life. His tiny part had been done and he must go. . . . He must be thrust out to make room for the more important. . . . Regarding himself as one of the unfit, he believed that nothing could accede for misery, a perception of this fact" (217).[3]

What is not entirely clear here in the discarded chapter 12 is how Crane himself is seeing what Henry says. Henry is being treated ironically, for without doubt he seeks something to blame for his situation other than himself and in so doing simply rationalizes. Does the fact of his rationalizing discredit the vehicle of his rationalization? The reference is to the theory of evolution, but what attitudes toward the theory are being expressed by Crane? The question is not easily answered. The irony directed against Henry consists in his illogical uses of the theory as when he applies his sense of the notion of survival of the fittest to his flight from battle. "If his life was being relentlessly pursued, it was not his duty to bow to the approaching death. Nature did not expect submission. On the contrary, it was his business to kick and bite and give blows as a stripling in the hands of a murderer. The law was that he should fight. He would be saved according to the importance of his strength" (215–16). To the reader it is clear that Henry is rationalizing at this point; it is not clear to Henry who applies "his findings to the incident of his flight from battle," concluding, "It was not a fault, a shameful thing; it was an act obedient to a law" (216). Henry breaks his train of thought when an antithetical notion enters his head, causing him to feel that his appeal to evolutionary theory does not solve his problem, for he continues to be subject to traditional values regarding proper conduct during battle: "But he was aware that when he had erected a vindicating structure of great principles, it was the calm toes of tradition that kicked it all down about his ears. He immediately antagonized then this devotion to the by-gone; this universal adoration of the past" (216). But even this anti-evolutionary stance Crane uses to shower irony upon Henry as he embraces the past at the exact same moment he rails against its influence on the present. He even goes so far as to see himself as a new Christ, clearly an indication of his own commitment to traditional values and a measure of his inability to be objective. "He resolved to reform it all. He had, presently, a feeling that he was the growing prophet of a world-reconstruction. Far down in the untouched depths of his being, among the hidden currents of his soul, he saw born a voice. He conceived a new world modelled by the pain of his life, and in which no old shadows fell blighting upon the temple of thought" (216).

Crane uses Henry's attitudes toward a Darwinistic nature in the discarded chapter 12 as a means of commenting on the limitations of Henry's maturation. His sense of being among the unfit as the result of the operation of forces over which he has no control causes him to rail against the operation of natural process: "It was a barbarous process with no affection for the man and the oak, and no sympathy for the rabbit and the weed" (217). Nature's indifference is not simply that but a *cruel* indifference, the irony lying in the fact that Henry should presume to judge what he has insufficient knowledge or evidence to judge. Such judgments simply reflect his character and state of mind. He asserts that though "powerless and at the will of law, he yet planned to escape; menaced by fatality he schemed to avoid it" (217). How can he possibly avoid the effects on him of the survival of the fittest? Obviously he cannot, a fact emphasized by his memory of a childhood episode at the conclusion of the discarded chapter 12. He recalls hiding in an empty flour barrel in his mother's pantry while his playmates search for him, and he imagines that in a similar way he can hide from fate in a place "where an all-powerful stick would fail to bruise his life. . . . He saw himself living in watchfulness, frustrating the plans of the unchangeable, making of fate a fool" (217–18). Without doubt, Crane intends in *The Red Badge* to invoke the Darwinistic scheme of nature. Henry Fleming seems to believe that scheme to be a true and valid description of the working of nature. Does Crane share his belief or is Henry's interpretation of nature another of his illusions? Since the answer to this question is so terribly complicated and involves so much of what remains to say about the novel, let us postpone the answer to this question until later. Meanwhile, we will examine the question of nature as Crane handles it in the novel as he finally intends it to be published.

The great number of references to animals, because so obvious, has been frequently noted.[4] The specific character of such references, however, has been less frequently noticed. Some of those references involve direct comparisons of men to animals either in metaphor or simile. People are like this particular animal in their behavior or like that particular animal. Other references involve indirect associations of human behavior with animal behavior, as when human actions are "dogged," people "howl," "squawk," "growl," or "snarl." Considered together, the direct references to animals, whether relating to specific or indirect comparison of human to animal behavior, fall within three categories: references to, and hence direct or implied comparisons between, people and domestic animals, wild animals, and mythological animals. In all there are approximately ninety instances of direct reference to specific animals (excluding simply mention of animal qualities as "eagle-eyed," or guns "roaring," use of the word *animal* when no specific animal is mentioned, and use of the word *beast* when no specific reference makes clear what kind of beast is meant).

The greatest number of references is to domestic animals, especially the horse. These are more negative in connotation than positive, and most frequently comparisons are either explicitly or implicitly made between qualities exhibited by people, Henry or his fellow soldiers, and qualities associated with animals. For example, at one point when Henry in the third chapter feels the impulse to warn his comrades of imminent danger, he thinks: "They must not all be killed like pigs." Crane means to do several things, chiefly to express far more meanings than Henry himself expresses from his limited perspective. First of all, he creates the association between people and animals, thus giving the comparison contextual meanings it would not carry in isolation. He then expresses Henry's literal meaning and all the connotations the word *pig* evokes. Finally he comments on Henry's character at this point in that Henry's observation is in context a false conclusion. Henry's fear for his own safety determines, as it so often does, how he sees and interprets the world around him. He is not concerned about the safety of the other men at all; rather his concern is, as nearly always, for himself alone. Henry's comment also indicates his own feeling that his situation is like that of a pig before slaughter. Subsequent events prove this assessment to be untrue. The most narrowly Darwinistic reading of the novel possible still leaves space for some modicum of control over one's destiny.

The domestic animal most frequently named in the text is the horse, not surprising in view of the fact that the horse was indeed used during the Civil War as the primary mode of individual transportation. If we look at the scenes in which horses appear, we see something other than the use of horses for realistic portrayal of war during the nineteenth century. Each time a horse appears in the novel there is a clearly established relation between horse and rider, man and animal. The first appearance of the horse is in chapter 2 where it is introduced in such a way as to suggest its thematic importance, revealing one of the possible relationships between humankind and nature. A kind of tableau is described whose relation to other scenes involving men and horses becomes clear once the question is raised: "In the eastern sky there was a yellow patch like a rug laid for the feet of the coming sun; and against it, black and patternlike, loomed the gigantic figure of the colonel on a gigantic horse" (22). Again various levels of meaning are presented here. Crane presents to us what appears before Henry's eyes; hence we see what Henry sees, but since Crane's vision is more comprehensive than Henry's, Crane's understanding of the meaning of what Henry sees is greater than Henry's. Crane's consciousness, as author, is more widely pervasive. Henry sees the tableau, but he is in no position to interpret its meaning in any kind of conscious way. It may well be implied that he has some subliminal understanding of its meaning, and for that reason it registers on his consciousness.

In any case the significant factor is that the man in the tableau is in charge of himself and his circumstances. The horse, symbolic in its giganticness of the power of nature, clearly stands in a position subordinate to that of the man, the colonel, its rider. The rider is in control and is hence capable of exerting such influence on nature as to control its power, to control the direction of the flow and the extent of its released energies. In the several scenes that follow in which men interact with horses, in every case what is emphasized is not the horse as mode of transportation, but as nature controlled by man, subject to human will. Always the control of the horse by the rider is emphasized as strong verbs tell what the rider does to control the horse: "A hatless general pulled his dripping horse to a stand near the colonel of the 304th. . . . You've got to hold 'em back! . . . . The general made a passionate gesture and galloped away" (40). There exists in this case a relationship between the authority of the rider over the horse and the authority of the rider over the circumstances in which he exists. This is so in all the scenes in which men are presented riding horses. If the individual riders are not themselves high-ranking officers, they are at least the emissaries of such, and their authority is reflected in their exertion of control: "A furious order [military order] caused commotion in the artillery. An officer on a bounding horse made maniacal motions with his arms" (49). And further: "A slim youth on a fine chestnut horse caught these swift words from the mouth of his superior. He made his horse bound into a gallop almost from a walk in his haste to go upon his mission" (50). The emphasis remains the same in each such scene: "As another officer sped his horse after the first messenger, the general beamed upon the earth like a sun. . . . His excitement made his horse plunge, and he merrily kicked and swore at it. He held a little carnival of joy on horseback" (51). Other such scenes depicting horses and riders in chapters 18 and 21 support similar readings. Emphasis is always on the rider's control of his horse rather than on the realistic presentation of an episode of war. The implication, insofar as humans are able to exert control over nature, is that consciousness plays some role in determining the direction of the movement of humans and that there is indeed a distinction to be made between people and animals, a distinction not so clear in the terms set out in Darwin's scheme of evolutionary development.

References to wild animals may be negative or positive as are the references to domestic animals. In both cases Crane's intention is to raise the question of the character of the relationship between humankind and nature. References to domestic animals are not all as positive as the horse symbol in that many of them suggest not the power of the horse but the powerlessness or weakness of the animal and, by analogy, humans. The cow, sheep, chicken, mule or jackass, kitten, and hen suggest weakness, passivity, stupidity, or other human limitations. Some of the references to untamed animals, such as those to the worm, rabbit, squirrel, and loon, carry similar connotations. But comparable to the use of the horse as a strong positive symbol are the many references to characteristics belonging to certain wild animals and attributed to humans. Fearlessness, strength, intrepidity are implied when people are said to be like the eagle, wolf, wildcat, or panther. Whereas the horse sets humankind apart from nature, some of the references to wild animals establish animal conduct as model for human conduct. Most references to wild animals, though, function simply to establish the similarity in general between humans and animals. Interestingly enough, in the last forty or so pages of the novel there are only six references to animals. All of these references are comparisons of human prowess to animal prowess.

We have already dealt with the significance of the references to mythological or fabulous animals. In actuality only three creatures are named—the monster, the dragon, and the serpent—though they are evoked with far more frequency than the number of times their names are used would suggest. Sometimes they are referred to by the use of pronouns, "they" or "them." When Henry feels that he or his regiment is going to be "gobbled," the reference must certainly be to one of these mythological creatures. Likewise when he feels he or his comrades are going to be "swallowed," there is a submerged reference to the largest animals named in the text, the dragons or monsters. When "in the darkness he saw visions of a thousand-tongued fear that would babble at his back and cause him to flee," he must have in mind the "monster" that he names in the next sentence (27–28). It is worth observing that references of this order diminish as the novel progresses, most of them occurring in chapters 2 to 6. There are no further such references in the final fifty or so pages of the text, and if we consider that the final reference is not an expression of trepidation on Henry's part but simply a memory of his having been afraid, then the use of any of these words as representing Henry's current fears disappears from the thirteenth to the final (twenty-fourth) chapter.

Crane's pervasive employment of figures of speech involving animals is only one element of his general interest in nature and in questions of an ultimately philosophical character revolving around the issue of the relation of humankind to nature. The opening paragraph of the novel describes the awakening army and the dawning day. Initially the reader feels that the scene is simply the description of an objective observer, an omniscient narrator, but that seems unsatisfactory given the third-person, limited, technical perspective of the novel as a whole. It seems unsatisfactory because the description is almost wholly subjective. That is, the change in temperature from cold to warmer is not in fact a "reluctant" change; it is simply a change involving no will of any kind as the word *reluctant* to the contrary implies. The landscape does not in fact "change from brown to green"; it only *seems* to. And the army does not in fact "tremble with eagerness"; it only seems an appropriate phrase to describe a general mood and atmosphere. There must undoubtedly be some in that body who are neither trembling nor eager. The river can only be a "*sorrowful* blackness" (my emphasis) to a very subjective observer. That observer, who also sees the enemy's campfires at night as emitting an "eyelike gleam," perhaps anticipating the images of dragons and monsters yet to come, is none other than Henry Fleming. In the very opening paragraph of the novel he begins to "read" nature, to interpret it in the light of his inner feelings, an enterprise in which he engages throughout the novel from the opening sentence to the final one.

A reader is not likely, however, on the first reading to understand fully the implications regarding nature contained in the first two chapters, at least not before Henry is moved for the first time to acknowledge and express feelings about his sense of his relationship to nature: "He lay down in the grass. The blades pressed tenderly against his cheek. The moon had been lighted and was hung in a treetop. The liquid stillness of the night enveloping him made him feel vast pity for himself" (25). The "blades" no more press "tenderly against his cheek" than the "cold" in the opening paragraph "passed reluctantly from the earth." Henry's reaction is to personify nature here as he personified the army at the novel's beginning. "Tenderness" implies the willed expression of positive emotion, and if the moon indeed "had been lighted" and "hung" in a tree, then some*one* must have lighted and hung it. Henry feels "pity" for himself and since the grass sympathizes with him and the moon has been lighted and hung for him, then nature must feel sympathy for him as well. And so it appears to: "There was a caress in the soft winds; and the whole mood of the darkness, he thought, was one of sympathy for him in his distress" (25). Who is this imagined "person" who expresses tenderness, hangs the moon in a treetop for him, caresses him and feels sympathy for him in his distress? It is the only female with whom he has experienced intimacy of the sort evoked here—his mother. In his imagination he fuses his own conception of nature with the memory of his own particular mother. Otherwise, what is the source of his sense of intimacy as described above? Hence the "mother nature" here is not some fabled, fairybook figure, but a creature emerged from the innermost recesses of his own consciousness and emotions.

We may feel reasonably safe in drawing this inference because of the association of ideas Henry makes during this scene. Immediately after his imagination has conjured up this intimation of mother nature, "He wished, without reserve, that he was at home again making the endless rounds from the house to the barn . . . he would have sacrificed all the brass

buttons on the continent to have been enabled to return to
[milk his cows]" (25–26). It is not simply his wish to return
home that establishes the connection in his mind between nature and mother but his recalling the particular memory of the
cows, of milking them, of anger toward them (as toward his
mother), of their function as a source of nourishment. In his
memory the cow displaces the figure of the mother, for he
does not have sufficient access to the content of his unconscious mind to realize that he wants to return to his mother at
this point. And if he did, he would hardly admit it—even to
himself—committed as he is to escaping from those bonds. Nature, then, stands in antithetical relation to the impulse driving
Henry to become, as he later phrases it, "a man of traditional
courage." How can this be? What sense does it make to see
nature as in some sense standing in direct opposition to Henry's
growth and development? At this point in the novel Henry is
clearly in conflict. His desire to leave home, join the army, and
to fight well in battle is frustrated by his lack of knowledge and
experience, his fear for his own safety and well-being, and his
apprehension that he might turn and flee. When he wishes that
he were home, thereby posing the possibility that he could resolve the dilemma by doing away with one of its poles (thus
eliminating the tension between the two impulses), Henry
firmly establishes the relation between involvement within the
sphere of nature and avoidance of the necessity of heroic action.
In other words, he is committed at once, perhaps alternately is
more precise, to nature, home, and mother and to their oppo-
sites, consciousness, independence, and individuation. In the
terms established by Crane in the novel, Henry must escape
from nature if he is to become "a man of traditional courage."
The notion of escaping from nature is not new in Western
thought. One of many paradigms of such movement available
to Crane is contained in Genesis, one of the chief myths of
Western culture. Though Crane obviously knew Genesis, as
suggested above, the pattern of relation between humankind

and nature projected there likewise appears in countless guises in Western thought, mythology, and literature. Though there are interesting parallels between the novel and Genesis, I would not claim that Crane derived his thought directly from that source.

9

Genesis and Darwinism

One way of interpreting Genesis is as an account not only of the origins of the universe, but also of the origins of human consciousness. The reader will recall that, according to the story, Adam and Eve are free to roam the Garden of Eden freely and to do anything that might occur to them *except* to eat of the fruit of the tree of knowledge of good and evil. They are allowed such freedom because their capacity to think and imagine is so limited that they cannot on their own conceive of acting independently of God. They have awareness but a very low level of consciousness, of the capacity to judge and make distinctions. Adam is told by God that he must not eat of the fruit of the tree of knowledge of good and evil, and if he does, he will die: "For in the day that thou eatest thereof thou shalt surely die" (2:17).[5] But He does not tell Adam all; the serpent tells the rest to Eve: when she eats the forbidden fruit, "ye shall be as gods, knowing good and evil" (3:5). This implies that Adam and Eve, though set above the animals in the natural hierarchy, yet belong to the sphere of nature, for they do not know good and evil. To know good and evil would remove them from sole existence in the sphere of nature because knowing good and evil bespeaks the facility to make a wide range of distinctions and hence to possess knowledge. A chief difference between gods and mortals before Adam's fall is that gods possess knowledge; mortals do not. As Eve sees it, eating the forbidden fruit will "make one wise" (3:6), will allow one to transcend the limitations of nature. Their access to higher consciousness comes to be as the result of their disobedience to God's will. Since consciousness allows the individual to distinguish himself from nature, from all other entities, Adam and Eve, in order to achieve higher consciousness, need to differentiate themselves from nature which they do through the exertion of will. At the same time, they separate themselves from God—distinguishing themselves from Him by setting their own wills against His and in effect challenging His authority.

Eating the forbidden fruit not only brings knowledge, wisdom, higher consciousness, and the ability to make distinctions and hence judgments, it also brings self-consciousness, guilt, and shame, and these components are not all clearly and easily separable. We know that consuming the forbidden fruit creates knowledge and higher consciousness because we are told that after they have both eaten it (note that higher consciousness occurs only after they have *both* [my emphasis] eaten it) "the eyes of them both were opened, and they knew that they *were* naked; and they sewed fig leaves together, and made themselves aprons" (3:7). Their knowledge consists in the fact that they are able to make distinctions they could not heretofore make. They knew, as they had not known before, that they were naked. Before they *knew* they were naked they had no awareness of it, and once they *know,* it is an occasion of shame. They have knowledge and are as the gods; yet their newfound advantage turns out to be a curse.

When they next encounter God, they act as they do because of their reaction to the first act of disobedience to God's will. Self-consciousness, guilt, and fear accompany higher consciousness. God's presence in the garden causes them to attempt to hide themselves. In response to God's call to him, Adam says that he has hidden himself because he is naked and was therefore afraid. Immediately God knows that Adam has eaten the forbidden fruit as indicated by his response to Adam's voice: "Who told thee that thou wast naked?" (3:11). God knows that previously Adam did not possess the self-consciousness to know of his nakedness. "Behold," God says, "the man is become as one of us, to know good and evil" (3:22). God expels Adam and Eve from the garden in order that they will no longer have access to the tree of life whose fruit would allow them eternal life. Hence death comes into the world, the twin of consciousness, for death's existence, the myth tells us, depends upon consciousness of it. Hence the truth of God's warning to Adam that if he eats the forbidden fruit, he will die. The serpent is right when he tells Eve she will not die, because he means she will not literally die upon tasting the fruit. Presumedly Adam and Eve would have died had the fall not occurred; otherwise God's motive for banishing them from the garden, so that they will not "take also of the tree of life and eat and live forever," does not make sense. Therefore death, according to the myth, is a matter of consciousness of it.

Henry's relation to nature is reflected in the myth's expression of the relation between humankind and nature. Initially there is complete and entire harmony between humankind and nature; Adam is at one with his natural environment, so much so that no enmity exists among the animals. The lion lies down with the lamb. But after the fall, as suggested by the eternal enmity God establishes between humans and serpent (Is this the serpent Henry imagines the enemy forces to be?), the disjunction occurs, and the enmity among the animals of the creation finds its genesis.

Specifically Henry's sense of his relationship with nature is expressed by his responses to his natural environment, especially when he sees the activities of humans against the background of nature. Consistently aware of nature during the course of the events of the novel, Henry interprets it alternately as nature from the perspective of Genesis or from the Darwinistic perspective. In the one case, nature is interpreted by Henry as both positive and negative: positive, meaning that he sees no disharmony and feels that nature is sympathetic and caring toward humans (as in the passage quoted above, "he lay down on the grass"); negative, meaning that nature is intentionally hostile, acting inimically so as to thwart human aims and aspirations. Nature in Genesis in its positive light is nature before the fall; in its negative light it is nature after the fall. Darwinistic nature (not necessarily as Darwin saw it but as his thought was interpreted) Henry sees as positive when he considers himself as one of the "fittest" and feels that his thoughts and actions correspond with the requirements for the survival of the fittest (its own kind of natural harmony); as negative when he considers himself a victim of nature, as unfit and without choice regarding his actions.

Although Genesis and the theory of evolution are evoked in the novel, it is not always easy nor possible to tell which scheme is operative at any given moment. For example, before Henry's first encounter with the enemy, "He thought that he did not relish the landscape. It threatened him" (31). A short time later an opposite response is elicited: "In the afternoon the regiment went out over the same ground it had taken in the morning. The landscape then ceased to threaten the youth. He had been close to it and become familiar with it" (34). If familiarity alone allays his fears, then his fears were not well grounded in the first place. As indeed they are not; the landscape itself should not be threatening but what the landscape holds. Is the reference here to the nature of Genesis or Darwin? Viewed from the perspective of Genesis, the situation may represent Henry as Adam before the fall in that Henry is the innocent who interprets nature as though he exists in intimate relation to it. The sense of conflict with nature, whereby nature seems to be an adversary when it threatens him, bespeaks Adam's relation with nature after the fall, though at this point Henry has undergone nothing comparable to the experience of the fall. At the same time the Darwinistic scheme may be evoked here in that Henry's fears stem from his fear that he is one of the unfit: "When, however, they began to pass into a new region, his fears of stupidity and incompetence reassailed him" (34).

At the conclusion of the fifth chapter, however, it is clear that Henry is then comparable to Adam before the fall. It is at the conclusion of the first encounter where he observes that "Nature" has not involved itself in such activity as he has been engaged in in fighting his first battle. Crane describes a very innocent and naive person: "As he gazed around him the youth felt a flash of astonishment at the blue sky and sun gleaming on the trees and fields. It was surprising that Nature had gone tranquilly on with her golden process in the midst of so much devilment" (45). The tone of the passage clearly implies that it should not be astonishing at all, that nature's process, whether golden or otherwise, has nothing to do with the affairs of humans. Chapter 17 ends similarly, but there it is not quite so clear how we should read it: "The forest still bore its burden of clamor. . . . Each distant thicket seemed a strange porcupine with quills of flame. A cloud of dark smoke, as from smoldering ruins, went up toward the sun now bright and gay in the blue, enameled sky (101). We know that these lines report what Henry sees at this time. The question is what is Henry's mood, attitude, thought? Where is he now? Is he seeing things any differently from the way he was seeing things at the end of chapter 5?

There are essentially three ways of interpreting this passage. One way is to see the lines as simply an observation of the results of human technology against a natural backdrop, creating, thereby, a contrast. In that case Henry, unlike in his observation at the end of chapter 5, is making a clear differentiation between the affairs of nature and the affairs of humankind. This becomes, then, a critique of Genesis, of the meaning of Adam's sense of his natural relation to his environment. In that sense the observation is a sign of growth and development, Henry having grown beyond the simple, naive sense that there exists a clear interrelationship between human behavior and natural process. The other way of interpreting the passage sees Henry as unable to perform the function of higher consciousness necessary to move beyond the point of development (or lack of it) indicated in the passage at the end of chapter 5. In this case he does not make the connection between the human activity and the natural activity, seeing them both as components of one large and continuous process. He simply sees but does not interpret the meaning of what he sees. He is as a camera, a medium of communication, whose function is simply to record. The third possibility of interpretation would insist that we cannot rest with either the first or the second, that neither can be strongly enough supported as to disqualify the other. No one of these interpretations clearly prevails. We are thus driven back to the text as a whole in order to determine the meaning of nature therein.

The central scene in *The Red Badge* having to do with nature occurs in chapter 7, the forest chapel scene. There Henry attempts to get as far away as he can from the battle he has just fled, and at the same time he wishes to retreat from all things the battle has meant to him, both consciously and unconsciously. He no longer wishes to fight in the war, to be a hero, to achieve maturity and autonomy. "He went from the fields into a thick wood, as if resolved to bury himself. He wished to get out of hearing of the crackling shots which were to him like voices" (52). He wishes, indeed, not that he were literally dead (though he has earlier felt that "He must look to the grave for comprehension" [35]), but that if he were buried, then he would have none of the problems that presently confront his conscious mind. He would like to be submerged in nature as the preconscious Adam was; he would like to become one with nature.

Whereas earlier he fantasized about a close sympathetic relation with nature ("The liquid stillness of the night enveloped him" [25]), he finally acts out that fantasy in his retreat from battle: "So he went far, seeking dark and intricate places" (52). Though nature seems not to welcome this return to the womb, she nonetheless responds particularly and specifically to him as an individual (or so Henry feels, at any rate). "The creepers, catching against his legs, cried out harshly as their sprays were torn from the barks of trees. The swishing saplings tried to make known his presence to the world. . . . When he separated embraces of trees and vines, the disturbed foliages waved their arms and turned their face leaves toward him" (52). Henry's attempt, it seems, is to bury himself in the very heart of nature, and once again he associates immersion in nature with total immersion within a woman, once again Mother Nature and probably on an unconscious level, as before when he thinks of home at a similar juncture, within his own mother, within the womb. "He conceived Nature to be a woman with a deep aversion to tragedy" (53). His attempt is again to read nature, to find in nature clues to justify, to vindicate his own conduct. That same landscape that not long ago threatened him now "gave him assurance" and rather than being a threat is "a fair field holding life" (53).

It is clear, however, that Henry reads nature only to his own advantage, only as he *wants* to read it. When he throws the pine cone at the squirrel and finds in the squirrel's response a sign, he sees it as "the law." What law requires the squirrel to run to escape danger? Darwin's law, the law of the survival of the fittest. The inferences Henry draws, "Nature had given him a sign" and "Nature was of his mind," contradict the notion of survival of the fittest, for nowhere in such a scheme is there place for any kind of sympathetic attachment between nature and humankind. On the contrary. In the world of Genesis nature may reveal signs, or more than that, nature can communicate directly with humans as the serpent does. But the one thing that distinguishes the serpent from his fellow beings is his mind, his subtlety, a quality that is his legacy to Adam and Eve and to the human race, the quality that forced the separation between humans and animals. The other natural phenomenon Henry sees immediately after the squirrel "gives him a sign" is a counter lesson. He sees "out at some black water, a small animal pounce in and emerge directly with a gleaming fish" (53). That too is no less a part of nature's operation, but the scene does not register. He does not read it because its implications, "nature red in tooth and claw," are not to his liking. Also it contradicts his impression rendered earlier during this scene that nature "would die if its timid eyes were compelled to see blood" (53).

The impression of Henry's movement within the forest is that as he gets further and further away from battle, he burrows deeper and deeper into nature, not only in a physical sense but also in a psychological sense. There is a merging during this episode of internal and external as Henry seems to perform actions reflecting the state of his interior being. One gets the sense that he is also burrowing into his own consciousness, seeking out what lies submerged, buried at its lower levels. The many reasons for seeing something womblike about the forest— Mother Nature, timid eyes, earlier associations between nature and femaleness—are compelling reasons to believe that Crane had in mind the idea of innocence, ignorance, and retrogression to some preconscious state of development on Henry's part. Henry reverts to the state of Adam before the fall, or at least tries to. What happens when he makes the supreme effort to return to the womb, to an earlier time, to innocence, is shown to us. The insight into human psychology, mythology, and philosophy revealed at this point in the novel cannot be overemphasized. "He walked on," we are told, "going from obscurity into promises of a greater obscurity" (53). The comment occurs when Henry reaches the forest chapel. In some senses this is the center of the novel, though there are several problems that arise if we identify this as the novel's climax or even central episode. Nonetheless Henry's movement from his entry into the forest to this crucial point in the narrative has seemed not aimless but purposeful. The "place where the high arching boughs made a chapel" (53) seems a destination. He has traveled through the wilderness until he reaches what is its center. It can only be, however, a "center" in some very subjective or metaphorical sense because, as we know, nature has no real, actual center (unless the center be God, in which case its center has location in neither time nor space—it is not a place to be traveled to). Hence this chapel must be a construction of Henry's own fabrication, clearly a chapel of the mind, even to its "green doors," and its "gentle brown carpet." He has not fancied *everything*. To be sure, Henry is indeed in the forest, he comes upon a clearing covered with pine needles, a not unusual scene in forests where pines grow. The "chapel," "green doors," "gentle brown carpet," and certainly the "religious half light" are of Henry's own making, projections from the interior of his psyche.

The corpse is actually there, not fantasized but real. Its meaning, however, is supplied by Henry, arising, as it does, out of his own thoughts, fears, needs, and feelings. The idea of chapel and religion is superimposed on nature in such a way as to suggest that Henry so interrelates them as to see nature and God as ultimately one. His excursion to the center of nature is expected to reveal that God is at the center of nature. Henry expects, as did Emerson before him, "to find God in the bush," to find at the center of nature "reason and faith." Instead, however, he finds death incarnate—not death in the abstract, but the actual, tangible, embodied vision of death in all its minutely detailed horror. And Henry's view, not a glance but a long look, reveals to him the most terrifying sight he has ever seen. Certainly the sight before him is one of the most grimly dismaying in all literature: "The corpse was dressed in a uniform that once had been blue, but was now faded to a melancholy shade of green. The eyes, staring at the youth, had changed to the dull hue to be seen on the side of a dead fish. The mouth was open. Its red had changed to an appalling yellow. Over the gray skin of the face ran little ants. One was trundling some sort of bundle along the upper lip" (53–54).

The minute detail and the tone in which it is recorded give the scene the appearance of objectivity, and it *is* objective, much like what a camera would record, except that the sight is described in such a way as to indicate Henry's participation in the observation. The red of the corpse's mouth, for example, has become an "appalling" yellow (to whom but to Henry?), and the eyes are not in fact staring at him; they only *appear* to be and to him alone. The grim details of the corpse's features contrast sharply with the expectations Henry brings to the scene. Interestingly enough, given as he is to looking for and interpreting signs from nature, he does not interpret this one in any conscious way. He reacts, however, and his reactions are in effect interpretations because he reacts in terms of the *meanings* the scene has for him. Basically his response is fear, a fear not essentially different from the fear he had imagined from the very beginning of the novel. As a matter of fact, we may see Henry's movement from the beginning of the novel as culminating in the forest chapel scene where he comes finally face to face with his innermost fears and trepidations.

The question arises as to what has happened by the time this scene ends at the conclusion of chapter 7. Has Henry entered into a new relationship with nature through his experience in the forest chapel? That is, does he understand that nature does not respond to him in any kind of personal way, does not give him signs? And does he understand that the meanings he projects onto nature are indeed projections, that nature is not his mother and does not sympathize with him? Or does he remain convinced that his relation to nature is that of the original relation that Adam and Eve had before the fall? In specific and particular terms we may ask whether Henry's response to the rotting corpse in the forest chapel signals another flight from his deepest fears or whether, when he "bursts the bonds which had fastened him to the spot and fled, unheeding the underbrush" (54), he is enacting a rebirth, the bonds being the umbilical bond—the link connecting the child with its mother, Henry with nature. In other words, something stands between the text and our clear apprehension of it.

Let me state the problem in yet another way. How should we read the concluding lines of chapter 7 and the opening lines of chapter 8? What is the meaning of the lines, "The trees about the portal of the chapel moved soughingly in a soft wind. A sad silence was upon the little guarding edifice" (54)? How should we read the beginning of chapter 8, the third sentence of the opening paragraph: "There was a lull in the noises of insects as if they had bowed their beaks and were making a devotional pause" (54)? Has Henry learned anything, or is he naively expressing again the attitude that there is a sympathetic and harmonious relationship between nature and humankind outside the scheme of Darwin? The source of the problem is the novel's tone, the attitudes, beliefs, and values of the narrator toward and regarding the ideas, subjects, and issues presented in the work. In this case the matter is complicated because we have two tones to deal with: the tone of the narrator and the tone of the character. The two are frequently in competition. The result is that we as readers struggle to know whose voice is the authoritative voice, the voice to be believed. This matter is so basic to the interpretation of *The Red Badge* because our sense of the meaning of the novel finally rests upon how we deal with the disparity between the two voices. The most essential meaning of the novel lies in the fact of conflict—the conflict between the perspectives of the narrator and his character; the conflict, ultimately, that forms the basis of all the conflict in the novel.

10

Tone of the Work

The problem of the duality of tone in *The Red Badge of Courage* is intensified because the tone of the narrator and that of the central character are not entirely at odds; they are only sometimes. We want to be able to distinguish between the occasions when Henry is deluding himself and when he is seeing things in a reasonable way. Central to our understanding of the novel is our interpretation of the meaning of Henry's "red badge." The scene during which he receives it stands in competition with the forest chapel scene as the center of the novel. As we have seen, the meaning of the forest chapel scene is ambiguous, but no less ambiguous is the meaning of Henry's "red badge of courage." The primary issue is whether or to what extent we are to see the symbol named in the book's title, the most significant symbol of the novel, as ironic. Had Henry actually been wounded in battle, there would be no problem; but as it is, a stigma attaches to the wound. Henry purposely lies when he tells his comrades that his wound is indeed a battle wound: "I got separated from the reg'ment. Over on the right, I got shot. In the head. I never see sech fightin' " (79–80). In such a circumstance as this, is the badge a badge of courage or a badge of shame? Perhaps at this point the reader will recall the question I raised earlier regarding whether Crane the author shares Henry's perspective on nature. By this time it is clear that the question is in truth a far more complex one: to what degree does Crane share Henry's perspective not only on nature but also on the meaning of his experience? The answer to the former question is an index to the answer to the latter. The novel's tone is the most essential element of its meaning. To understand its tone is to understand what the novel means. There are, however, fortunately or otherwise, barriers to the clear and unequivocal apprehension of the meaning of the tone.

It might be worthwhile to gauge the novel's tone by reference to our sense of the degree of sympathy existing between narrator and character and, hence, finally, author and character. The question then becomes one of determining when the author (through his agent the narrator) looks at Henry with sympathy and when he considers Henry a fool, a dupe, a victim of his own naiveté. This is sometimes relatively simple, sometimes not. The problem is in making the overall assessment. Sometimes the narrator is clearly ironic; sometimes there is a clear disparity between the attitude of the author and that of the character. At other times, crucial times, there is no disparity. There exists, for example, some degree of ironic treatment of Henry between the forest chapel scene and the conclusion of the novel, but it is clear that the irony diminishes after the forest chapel to the extent that it is nonexistent in the scenes where it seems that Henry is proving himself to be a "man of traditional courage." When he becomes the color-bearer, and when he consciously and intentionally exposes himself to the danger of his own annihilation, there is no ironic tone present. We see, in fact, a person who is firmly in conscious control of his emotions and instincts; we see one who is human and not the squirrel who gave Henry conduct lessons earlier.

As the novel moves toward its close, however, the irony

reappears, and the reader's problem then becomes how to balance the positive and negative attitudes expressed through the narrator toward Henry. The problem seems to be complicated by Crane himself, especially through his editorial alterations. After many pages of non-ironic rendition of his narrative, the narration suddenly becomes not only ironic but *heavily* ironic. I have already pointed out the significance of the sentence, "He saw that he was good" (p. 47 above). Let me point again to an example of the extraordinarily heavy irony that Crane removed from the novel prior to its publication. Those deletions help to establish the meaning of the novel and are finally not confusing or contradictory at all. The key to the novel's meaning lies in the balance between what Crane left in the novel and what he took out. A particular sentence, as it appeared in the original manuscript, is a clear emblem of his original intention. That sentence quoted before in another context, its deleted phrase bracketed, is the following: "He had been to touch the great death, and found that, after all, it was but the great death [and was for others]" (134). The point to be made here is that the deleted phrase forces an ironic reading of the sentence, and by removing it Crane diminishes the possibility that the reader will interpret the novel as totally ironic. Crane did not delete *all* of the irony of the concluding pages, though he deleted most of it, especially the heavily, clearly, and most unambiguously ironic passages.

The concluding sentence of the novel (the third ending which Crane gave it, suggesting strongly that he had given much thought and attention to it), "Over the river a golden ray of sun came through the hosts of leaden rain clouds," reads considerably less ironically than it read before Crane removed so much of the final chapter's irony. Specifically, one of the ironic passages Crane expunged is one clearly inviting us to read the novel as ironic. "The imperturbable sun shines on insult and worship. As he was thus fraternizing again with nature . . ." (132). Were Henry indeed "again fraternizing with nature," it would indicate that no growth or development has occurred, that he has not grown but is as deluded at the end of the novel as when he threw the pine cone at the squirrel. That is the point when he most clearly and at length "fraternizes with nature." The novel's final sentence is so masterful because it reads exactly as Crane intended: It is so contrived that it does not reveal with certainty whether Henry is finding information about himself in nature, reading nature, or whether he is simply observing what appears before him. Does he feel that the "golden ray of sun" and the "leaden rain clouds" have anything to do with his life? We cannot tell.

Were the novel to be read as the traditional novel of heroism, it would suggest that Crane supports the values that have traditionally defined heroism, maturity, and identity. Read as ironic and as presenting Henry as deluded, the novel undercuts traditional definitions of heroism (and tradition in general) and points to the subjective and social character of human values. To put the issue in other terms, we might say that one reading supports a traditional, religious (in its most general sense), mythological view of the universe and humankind's relation to it; the other supports a contrary view, the view that the implications of the Darwinistic interpretation of nature and the universe are the most satisfactory way of knowing and understanding. One meaning admits human will as vitally instrumental in determining the nature and destiny of the individual; the other at least calls into question the role and efficacy of will in the conduct of life. I do not believe, however, that either way of reading the novel is satisfactory, for each reading is equally supported by substantial textual evidence, and each, of course, by definition refutes the other.

The implication is, therefore, that both readings are equally valid and equally invalid. Neither has the status of truth; both have the status of truth. The text will allow neither to be dismissed, for the contexts in which they exist allow the possibility of the truth of both. In the universe created in the novel there is no place to stand that will afford an adequate vantage point from which to judge which of the perspectives presented is, from the author's viewpoint, the more viable. Assuming that the author intends this state of affairs since he has gone to such great lengths to bring it about, we are inclined to ask what can the novel mean?

Crane's novel reflects the problem resulting from the diminishment of the authority of traditional institutions, especially the church, and the failure of any entity to buttress diminished institutional authority. Science was the main culprit, beginning mainly with Copernicus in the sixteenth century, continuing with Galileo in the seventeenth, and Newton in the eighteenth. The effect of their scientific effort was to demonstrate that traditional notions of the relation between humankind, nature, and the universe were not those that Scripture and common sense defined. Darwin in the mid-nineteenth century continued the line of thought and reason that, though not intended specifically by him, had probably the greatest role in undermining the religious authority enjoyed by the Christian church for many centuries for he raised serious questions about creation and hence the very foundations of Christianity. The result was not only to undermine religious authority but also to undermine the authority of all other institutions depending upon religion for support. Crane knew that the basis of all knowledge had been challenged and stood on the brink of a radical alteration of thought in his time. He knew that the very authority that traditionally defined for us who we are and how we stand in relation to universal process, our very identities, no longer held sway to the extent that it once had. Religion no longer had the power to contain and control the character and nature of knowledge in the way that it could when it could burn a heretic at the stake or force a thinker to renounce his nonconforming thought. Religion could no longer mold knowledge so easily to its needs.

Crane somehow or other understood all this, and he had

some understanding of its implications. He knew, perhaps an inference drawn from his own life experience, that as institutional authority waned, the reliance of the individual upon his own private and subjective knowledge and understanding, on his own view of the world, waxed. He understood the problems attendant upon simple acceptance of authority. Specifically, he saw as problematic that one's identity should be defined by the authority of traditional modes of definition. He felt, to be even more specific, that Henry should discover who he is, not in the preexistent terms of myth, but in his own terms. "He felt that in this crisis his laws of life were useless. Whatever he had learned of himself was here of no avail. He was an unknown quantity. He saw that he would again be obliged to experiment. . . . He must accumulate information of himself . . ." (18). To prove himself, "he must have blaze, blood, and danger, even as a chemist requires this, that, and the other" (21).

At the same time, he is aware of the limitations and dangers of the individual's reliance totally and entirely, in the extreme case, on his own resources. If one does not check his perceptions and inferences against those of others, it is entirely possible that one may begin to see in a totally idiosyncratic way. We see Henry doing this. When he sees himself as superior to the rest of mankind, even to the extent that he thinks of himself as God or Jesus, we may be sure that he is deluded, especially since his extreme subjectivity drives him toward easy identification with a supposedly "objective reality," a mythological scheme whose reality depends upon the authority supporting it and not upon the experience of the individual at all. There are dangers in striking out against authority; being entirely on one's own.

The result of his awareness of the issues outlined above did not cause confusion in Crane's mind, for the careful reader will note that Henry Fleming is far more the traditionalist than the narrator, through whom Crane presents by means of an ironic tone the alternative to his way of seeing things. Both visions are clearly presented textually, and there is not the slightest hint that the narrator is confused, nor, for that matter, is Henry Fleming. He might be deluded, but he is not confused. He is perfectly clear about what he thinks and believes. He might even be mistaken, but when we see him in the final stages of the book, he is not confused.

Crane by virtue of presenting the opposing perspectives does not signal that he sees them as possessing equal value. Though he presents the traditional view, it is clear that the nontraditional view has the more authoritative presentation. As pointed out earlier, the narrator's voice is more authoritative than Henry's because the narrator clearly knows more than Henry, is far more sophisticated and capable of rendering accurate judgments. In the presentation of the two views Crane seems to have in mind the realistic portrayal of a normal and balanced psyche. He is not conducting a debate between Darwinism and Christianity, between radicalism and conservatism. He presents finally a perspective that is more sympathetic toward the naturalistic perspective, but is not entirely free from the influence of more traditional views. He presents something of the way of seeing things expressed in several of his poems in which he sees God not as nonexistent, as a completely naturalistic view would require, but as cold, cruel, or uncaring. To say "God is cold" as he writes in "A man adrift on a slim spar" is a far cry from "God is dead," and even that implies that He once lived. Crane's mind is a complex one and his novel, *The Red Badge of Courage*, reflects that complexity in its most brilliant manifestation.

Notes

1. Quoted by R. W. Stallman in *Stephen Crane: A Critical Bibliography* (Ames: Iowa State University Press, 1972), ix.

2. A list of such critics would include most who have written about the novel and would be a long list indeed. A representative sample of critics who argue the question is contained in Stanley B. Greenfield, "The Unmistakable Stephen Crane," *PMLA* 73 (December 1958):562–63, 568–72.

3. The quotations cited here from the expunged chapter 12 are taken from the extant pages reprinted in R. W. Stallman's edition of the novel from which all subsequent quotations in this chapter derive.

4. I call attention particularly to Mordecai and Erin Marcus, "Animal Imagery in *The Red Badge of Courage*," *Modern Language Notes* 74 (1959), 108–11.

5. Chapter and verse from Genesis, King James version of the Bible, are cited in parentheses.

Bibliography

Primary Sources

The authoritative text of Crane's complete works is *The Works of Stephen Crane,* edited by Fredson Bowers, Charlottesville: University Press of Virginia, 1969–76.

Novels

Maggie: A Girl of the Streets (A Story of New York), by Johnston Smith [pseud.]. New York: N. p. 1893.

The Red Badge of Courage: An Episode of the American Civil War. New York: D. Appleton & Co., 1895.

George's Mother. New York and London: Edward Arnold, 1896.

The Third Violet. New York: D. Appleton & Co., 1897.

Active Service. New York: Frederick A. Stokes Co., 1899.

The O'Ruddy: A Romance. New York: Frederick A. Stokes Co., 1903. Completed after Crane's death by Robert Barr.

Shorter Fiction

The Little Regiment and Other Episodes of the American Civil War. New York: D. Appleton & Co., 1896.

The Open Boat and Other Stories. London: William Heinemann, 1898.

The Monster and Other Stories. New York and London: Harper & Brothers, 1899.

Whilomville Stories. New York and London: Harper & Brothers, 1900.

Wounds in the Rain: War Stories. New York: Frederick A. Stokes Co., 1898.

Last Words. London: Digby, Long & Co., 1902.

Bibliography

Other Editions

Follett, Wilson. *The Works of Stephen Crane*. New York: Alfred A. Knopf, 1925–27. 12 vols.

Gullason, Thomas A. *The Complete Short Stories and Sketches of Stephen Crane*. New York: Doubleday & Co., 1963.

———. *The Complete Novels of Stephen Crane*. New York: Doubleday & Co., 1967.

Levenson, J. C. *The Prose and Poetry of Stephen Crane*. The Library of America. New York: Literary Classics of the United States, 1984.

Katz, Joseph. *The Poems of Stephen Crane*. New York: Cooper Square Publishers, 1966.

Stallman, R. W. *Stephen Crane: An Omnibus*. New York: Alfred A. Knopf, 1952.

———. Sullivan County Tales and Sketches. Ames: Iowa State University Press, 1968.

——— and Lillian Gilkes. *Stephen Crane: Letters*. New York: New York University Press, 1960.

——— and E. R. Hagemann. *The New York City Sketches of Stephen Crane and Related Pieces*. New York: New York University Press, 1966.

Secondary Sources

Bibliographies

Beebe, Maurice, and Thomas A. Gullason. "Criticism of SC: A Selected Checklist with an Index to Studies of Separate Works." *Modern Fiction Studies* 5:282–91.

Cady, Edwin H. Selected Bibliography. *Stephen Crane*. New York: Twayne Publishers, 1962. Pp. 169–80.

Leary, Lewis. *Articles on American Literature: 1950–67*. Durham, N. C.: Duke University Press, 1970.

Stallman, R. W. *Stephen Crane: A Critical Bibliography*. Ames: Iowa State University Press, 1972.

Wertheim, Stanley. "Stephen Crane." In *Hawthorne, Melville, Stephen Crane: A Critical Bibliography*. New York: Free Press, 1971, Pp. 200–301.

Books

Ahnebrink, Lars. *The Beginnings of Naturalism in American Fiction*. Uppsala, Sweden: A. B. Lundequistka Bokhandeln, 1950. The earliest and among the best of the studies of Crane and naturalism.

Bassan, Maurice, ed. Introduction to *Stephen Crane: A Collection of Critical Essays*. Englewood Cliffs, N. J.: Prentice Hall, 1967. A useful collection encompassing a broad spectrum of views on Crane.

Beer, Thomas. *Stephen Crane: A Study in American Letters*. New York: Alfred A. Knopf, 1923. The first biography. Its intention is largely to correct the popular notion of Crane as immoral, an alcoholic, and a drug addict. Heavily psychological in its interpretations of Crane's life and work.

Berryman, John. *Stephen Crane*. New York: William Sloane Associates, 1950. A psychological study of Crane's life and an analysis of his fiction and poetry in relation to his life.

Cady, Edwin H. *Stephen Crane*. New York: Twayne Publishers, 1962. Especially valuable for its conservative but sensible readings of Crane's work.

Colvert, James B. *Stephen Crane*. (H. B. J. Biographies) New York: Harcourt Brace, 1984. There is no new information in this biography, but it contains most of the available photographs of Crane.

Gibson, Donald B. *The Fiction of Stephen Crane*. Carbondale, Ill.: Southern Illinois University Press, 1968. An analytical reading of all of Crane's major fiction, both short stories and novels.

Gullason, Thomas A. *Stephen Crane's Career: Perspectives and Evaluations*. New York: New York University Press, 1972. Extremely useful collection of documents detailing the evolution of Crane's career and reputation.

Hoffman, Daniel G. *The Poetry of Stephen Crane*. New York: Columbia University Press, 1957. The first and most extensive full-scale analysis of Crane's poetry.

LaFrance, Marston. *A Reading of Stephen Crane*. New York and London: Oxford University Press, 1971. Asserts that Henry achieves psychological maturity by the novel's end.

Nagel, James. *Stephen Crane and Literary Impressionism*. University Park: Pennsylvania State University Press, 1980. The most extended treatment of the question of impressionism in Crane's work.

Solomon, Eric. *Stephen Crane: From Parody to Realism*. Cambridge, Mass.: Harvard University Press, 1966. The book's thesis is that Crane's style has its origins in his parodying of contemporary popular fiction.

Stallman, R. W. Introductions and Notes to *Stephen Crane: An Omnibus*. New York: Alfred A. Knopf, 1952. This is the book chiefly responsible for the modern interest in Crane.

Bibliography

————. *Stephen Crane: A Biography*. New York: George Braziller, 1968. The definitive biography of its subject.

Walcutt, Charles C. *American Literary Naturalism: A Divided Stream*. Minneapolis: University of Minnesota Press, 1956. The most intelligent, able, imaginative treatment of American naturalism.

Articles

Albrecht, Robert C. "Content and Style in *The Red Badge of Courage*." *College English* 28(1966):487–92. A study attempting to bridge the gap between meaning and technical perspective.

Binder, Henry. "*The Red Badge of Courage* Nature Knows." *Studies in the Novel* (North Texas State University) 10(1978):i, 9–47 The deletions from the original manuscript cause the novel's ending not to make sense.

Breslin, Paul. "Courage and Convention: *The Red Badge of Courage*." *Yale Review* 66:209–22. Henry does become courageous even though that courage is grounded in illusion.

Burhans, Clinton S., Jr. "Judging Henry Judging: Point of View in *The Red Badge of Courage*." *Ball State University Forum* 15(1974):38–48. Points out the complexity of the problem of point of view in the novel and the humor of much of its irony.

Colvert, James B. "Stephen Crane's Magic Mountain." In *Stephen Crane: A Collection of Critical Essays*, edited by Maurice Bassan, 95–105. Englewood Cliffs, N. J.: Prentice Hall, 1967. Traces the "flaw" of the novel's ending to Henry's conception of himself and the exaggerated scope of his problem.

Cox, James T. "The Imagery of *The Red Badge of Courage*." *Modern Fiction Studies* 5(1959):209–19. Through the course of the narrative Henry develops awareness of the true character of the universe.

Fraser, John. "Crime and Forgiveness: *The Red Badge of Courage* in Times of War." *Criticism* 9(1967):243–56. Explores the moral implications of the novel.

Fryckstedt, Olov. "Cosmic Pessimism in Stephen Crane's *Red Badge of Courage*." *Studia Neophilologica* 32(1961):265–81. Underlying the events of the novel is reflected Crane's belief in the ultimate meaninglessness of everything.

Greenfield, Stanley B. "The Unmistakable Stephen Crane." *Publication of the Modern Language Association* 73(1958):562–72. Crane's view of the meaning of things is a dual view and critics mistakenly interpret his work unless they take this into account.

Hart, John E. "*The Red Badge of Courage* as Myth and Symbol." *University of Kansas City Review* 19(1953):249–56. Henry Fleming's discovery of self and his relation to the group in the novel follows the pattern of development of the hero of mythology.

Ives, C. B. "Symmetrical Design in Four of Stephen Crane's Stories." *Ball State University Forum* 10(1969):i, 17–26. Sets out to define the structure of the novel in terms of symmetrical design.

Kwiat, Joseph. "Stephen Crane and Painting." *American Quarterly* 4 (1952):331–38. Deals with the thorny problem of the relation of Crane's style to contemporary art.

McDermott, John J. "Symbolism and Psychological Realism in *The Red Badge of Courage.*" *Nineteenth Century Fiction* 23(1968):324–31. The apparent contradictions of the novel result from Crane's employment of psychological realism.

Mailloux, Stephen. "*The Red Badge of Courage* and Interpretive Conventions: Critical Response to a Text." *Studies in the Novel* (North Texas State University) 10(1978):i, 48–63. The deletions from the original text of the novel obscure what would otherwise be its clear meaning.

Pease, Donald. "Fear, Rage, and the Mistrials of Representation in *The Red Badge of Courage.*" In *American Realism: New Essays,* edited by Eric Sundquist, 155–75. Baltimore: Johns Hopkins University Press, 1982. Through the novel Crane repudiates authorized versions of the meaning of war in privileging experiences alien to that version and to traditional war narratives.

Rathbun, John W. "Structure and Meaning in *The Red Badge of Courage.*" *Ball State University Forum* 10(1969):8–16. The structure of the novel is revealed by attention to its narrative continuity which in turn yields its meaning.

Shroeder, John. "Stephen Crane Embattled." University of Kansas City Review, 17(1950):119–29. The major theme, Henry's relation to nature, fails to be resolved because of Crane's confusion at the conclusion.

Vanderbilt, Kermit, and Daniel Weiss. "From Rifleman to Flagbearer: Henry Fleming's Separate Peace in *The Red Badge of Courage.*" *Modern Fiction Studies* 11(1965-1966):371–80. The central episode of the novel occurs when Henry wrenches the flag from the hands of the dying flag-bearer.

Van Meter, Jan. "Sex and War in *The Red Badge of Courage*: Cultural Themes and Literary Criticism." *Genre* 7(1974):71–90. A thoroughly Freudian reading of the novel which sees the novel's conflicts as sexual in nature.

Index

Ahnebrink, Lars, 15
American Literature (journal), 14
Appleton, D. & Co. (publishing house), 12, 13
Anderson, Sherwood, 14

Bacheller syndicate, 48
Beer, Thomas, *Stephen Crane: A Study in American Letters* (biography), 13
Beginnings of Naturalism in American Fiction, The. See Lars Ahnebrink
Berryman, John, 15
Brooks, Cleanth, 14

Carnegie, Andrew, 3
Cather, Willa, 14
Civil War, 3
Conrad, Joseph, 13, 14
Copernicus, 97
Crane, Stephen, and convention and tradition, 2, 4, 8–9, 12, 59, 99; his literary language; literary reputation of, 13–16; WORKS: (poetry) "A Man Adrift on a Slim Spar," (posthumous poem), 99; *The Black Riders*, analysis of poem in, 51–52; first publication of, 8; philosophy in, 9; religion in, 9; style, 9;

WORKS: (prose) "An Experiment in Misery," characters in, 2; *Maggie: A Girl of the Streets*, characters in, 2; Darwinism in, 71; republication, 8; and literary tradition, 8–9; nature in, 69; mentioned by Howells, 11; "The Men in the Storm," characters in, 2; *The Red Badge of Courage*, animal references in, 74–78; and authority, 6, 24, 29, 83, 97, 98; Bacheller syndicate, 48; circularity of plot, 35–36; conflict in, 19–37, 80, 92; consciousness, 29–30, 32–33; fear, 20, 28–34, 41, 47, 50, 91; editions of, 16; first publication, 8; guilt, 41, 47, 83; Henry Fleming's mother, 22–25, 61, 79–80, 88, 91; heroism in, 7, 25, 28, 45–59, 96; historical context, 2–4; irony, 38–44, 50–59, 63–64, 71–73, 94–95; Jim Conklin, 35, 60–61, 71; "the lieutenant," 44, 49; and literary history, 5–6, 7; myth and fairytale in, 7, 21–22, 26, 31, 45–47, 50, 57, 63, 98; names of characters, 48–49; narrator in, 5, 7, 48, 53–54,

Index

About the Author

Donald B. Gibson received his B.A. and M.A. degrees from the University of Kansas City (subsequently the University of Missouri at Kansas City). He completed his Ph.D. at Brown University in 1962. He taught for a year as an instructor at Brown before leaving to teach at Wayne State University, Detroit, in the fall of 1961. In 1964 he received a Fulbright award to Jagiellonian University, Cracow, Poland, where he taught American literature for two years. He returned to the United States in 1966 and the following year was appointed associate professor of English at the University of Connecticut and Professor in 1970.

His interest in black American writers intensified during this time and to his publication of *The Fiction of Stephen Crane* in 1968 he added "The Negro: An Essay on Definition," *Yale Review*, March 1968. Subsequently he published *Five Black Writers: Essays on Wright, Ellison, Baldwin, Hughes, and LeRoi Jones* and *Modern Black Poets* (both edited volumes), *The Politics of Literary Expression* (1981) and other volumes and articles, notably "Reconciling Public and Private in Frederick Douglass's *Narrative*," *American Literature* (1985).

Since 1974 he has been distinguished professor of American literature at Rutgers University, New Brunswick, New Jersey.